ISBN 978-1-330-55490-6
PIBN 10077952

English
Français
Deutsche
Italiano
Español
Português

www.forgottenbooks.com

Mythology Photography **Fiction**
Fishing Christianity **Art** Cooking
Essays Buddhism Freemasonry
Medicine **Biology** Music **Ancient**
Egypt Evolution Carpentry Physics
Dance Geology **Mathematics** Fitness
Shakespeare **Folklore** Yoga Marketing
Confidence Immortality Biographies
Poetry **Psychology** Witchcraft
Electronics Chemistry History **Law**
Accounting **Philosophy** Anthropology
Alchemy Drama Quantum Mechanics
Atheism Sexual Health **Ancient History**
Entrepreneurship Languages Sport
Paleontology Needlework Islam
Metaphysics Investment Archaeology
Parenting Statistics Criminology
Motivational

BY THE SAME AUTHOR

Sent post-paid at the above prices

The Liberty Press, Boston, Mass., U. S. A.

THE HORROBOOS

BY

MORRISON I. SWIFT

472.50

THE LIBERTY PRESS

BOSTON, 1911

To M.

CONTENTS

THE HORROBOOS

CHAPTER I

Colonel Fessenden Brady

It was the last night of the century and a number of us had gathered to witness the closing heart-beat of a hundred years. To while away the time until the ancient patient's demise we began to tell stories, drawing on our imaginations so vigorously that in some cases it seemed that the faculty might never be quite elastic again. There was among us one who did not yield himself to our sprightly vein, who indeed, if we were to speak from his reveried air, hardly felt the bracing sallies of mirth which gathered into spirited gales in their passage from mind to mind. At length we bantered him on his taciturnity, voting that he too must lay a story upon the altar of laughter. "Greyson! Greyson!" cried several, whereupon we all shuffled our chairs making him the center.

I am not a person of flaming fancy, began the gentleman thus importuned, and if you demand improvisation I shall humbly vacate the office of amusement to which you have elected me. Moreover, upon this of all nights of my life I am chilled with sombre memories which hold my mind in their unrelenting grasp. What I shall tell you is true—would it were not!—true even to the indelible language I shall repeat, and occurred ten years ago at this very hour. Although never have I spoken of it to a living being, not a day has passed when I have not earnestly meditated upon my part in it; it has weighed too heavily on my mind; with the new century I am resolved to throw its shadowy incubus off and be again a free gay-hearted man.

I was returning from Europe on one of the great liners. We had reached mid-ocean on the last day of the year and were plowing through storming seas which kept the majority in bed; but seven or eight of us, all men of course, who had formed an agreeable companionship by talking most of the time together in the smoking room, whetting our appetites for stories, smoke, and genial ocean follies by transitory conflicts with the sleety blasts on deck, conspired to make a midnight of it, to co-operate with the first rocking of the new year in the cradle of the sea. Finding the smoking-room pretty much deserted before nine o'clock, we took possession of our favorite corner and began to yarn. Rather more champagne than usual having been drunk in honor of the great proceeding of nature, our narratives took on a vividly human, personal, and autobiographical character. It must have been the feeling of old and confidential friendship engendered by wine and boreal song that moved Colonel Fessenden Brady, a highly entertaining gentleman, but one in the lambent ether of whose nature could be discerned the haughty cleavages of dignity and reserve, to give us a singular chapter from his own life. Brady was a world-nobleman before whose stateliness I wondered at the audacity of nature to storm,—handsome, polished, majestical, magnificently dressed, oracular, perfect, and aureoled in the spiritual majesty of fabulous wealth. This was his story.

A few years ago I went out to Africa for the first time as a missionary.

As a missionary! we ejaculated, and all joined in a courteous laugh at this cheerful thrust. Attracted by the word missionary, or Africa, or by our restrained hilariousness, a dark young splendid looking person, garbed in surpassing elegance, with a fortune of gold and two of diamonds visible on his dazzling exterior, lounged toward us and sat condescendingly down. Colonel Brady continued.

I expected you to smile, but it is the glittering truth; I went out there as a missionary, which I don't think you find harder to believe of me than I do of myself. This was the manner of it: I was looking about New York for a way to become a multimillionaire in two years at farthest, as all well-born and true-hearted American youths will, and I wasn't finding it very fast, when the idea possessed me that the smoothest road to my deserved estate lay through a new country, undesecrated by greed. Shunning books of travel and other beaten tracks through the wilderness, I haunted the water front, sailors' homes and boarding houses, and the little religious camps in the maritime desert, leeching myself on to every human oddity whose corroded exterior indicated foreign adventure, with whom I put myself on terms of brotherly familiarity. Fortune was certainly enamored of me, for I came upon a friendless wretch in the last stages of poverty and consumption who changed the destinies of my life. I helped him with small sums, always being repaid at sight with compound affection, and was soon gratified to perceive that for novel experience concerning wild tribes, unknown localities, dark deeds and suppressed information he was a noble gem out-shining all competitors, into whose deeps I cautiously probed for the great secret of which such a character could not be destitute.

I wooed his confidence with gruel and credulity, where his dying memory flagged I stimulated it with draughts of my own sparkling fancy, and often I talked obliquely, as if he had already told me everything, to surprise him into some fertile hints. But I never caught him that way, for he was a shrewd quill; it was my indefatigable kindness, not my wit, and the plain pounding of death on his ribs within that conquered. A few days before dying he com-

municated what I sought. With two dare-devil companions
he had forced his way some distance inland from the
African coast by untried routes until they had ascended to
a small tribe occupying a rich and protected basin among
the hills. These savages, who called themselves Rinyos,
and were a twin half of the great Horroboo nation, as I
later learned, altho cannibals and tumultuously warlike,
were nevertheless highly intelligent for their kind, if not
too openly abused were agreeably tame, and were mild and
lovable in their domestic relations when their wives were
obedient. Their most engaging attribute was the gold that
stocked their country and of which they were abjectly, I
may say sinfully, ignorant. After a brief visit the adventurers had departed uninjured, determined either to sell
their secret for a huge sum or to return with suitable support to exploit the treasure. On their journey coastward
they became mutually suspicious, which distemper, fed by
unsanitary climatal influences, grew rapidly into a madness,
so that none of them dared to sleep for fear of treachery.
Nor would they trust one another to separate, each believing that whoever emerged from the brush first would forestall the others and reap the entire harvest. Of course this
could not last long: two of them one day fell foul of each
other, and as they fought my acquaintance dispatched both
as security for his own life and clean title to the Horroboo
section of Africa.

From the dying man I obtained a minute description of
the parts he had traversed; I faithfully tended him to the
last, that he might not in his final agony chatter of his
peregrinations to strangers, and when his latest breath was
drawn I hurriedly turned him over to the city for burial,
and addressed myself to weightier affairs. I can assure you
I lost no time in planning to gather in these revealed truths,
as I called them from evangelical habit,—for what after
all is doctrinally truer in this world than dollars?—nor was

it long before a thousand infallible schemes crowded my consciousness, lacking only the fell essential of funds for their execution. Here I was in deep distress; my little savings from theological prizes, scholarships and small gifts intended for the Lord from pious rich women, were fast gliding away, while, pessimistic of the virtues of mankind, the idea of taking some capitalist into partnership to lie on his couch and absorb the spoils garnered by my brain, muscle and sacrifices, was, I must say, intolerably repulsive. Drooping in this sorry state for many days, I happened to receive an invitation to preach in a small town, and in the twinkling of an eye my worries vanished. I resolved to go to the African tribe as a missionary. As such my passage out would be paid and I could find myself in money from the Church or benevolent individuals to supply the materials which my plan involved.

You are probably wondering why I was invited to preach. In the middle of my college course my father met with reverses which would have terminated my education had not a wealthy trustee whose specialty was recruiting the ministry offered funds for the balance of my studies if I would then equip for the church. Joyfully I accepted, with very little intention as you may imagine of ever preaching. I saw however that under the wing of this wealthy citizen I should be brought into favorable relation with affluent men of influence, the controllers of worldly openings; so having passed through college and the seminary—the latter by an excellent head for theology cutting down to two years —I found myself distressed with doctrinal scruples which prevented the examining board from confirming the privilege to preach. This honorably excused me from a tasteless and impecunious profession, somewhat diluted in moral stamina, I fear, and I had my four years of education free. As the new call to preach arose from a more liberal body, I should have been constrained to widen the range of my

conscience to other perplexities, had it not given me the
glorious opening into the missionary arena. Laying my
plan before the denomination's foreign board, which was
that I should proceed alone into this dangerous field, I
became in an hour their religious lion, and the needful
money was poured into my pockets while blessings streamed
upon my head at an equal rate. To be frank, as it was
generally expected that I would be summarily eaten, the
virtue of my martyrdom was expected to be diffused among
my senders; and anticipating this rich and speedy return
for their acts, the good people felt eager to do handsomely
toward my comfort by liberal preparation for the few
months that I had to live.

My equipment was not just what they imagined it to be,
and I did not publicly advertise its character. That severe
array of strong well-braced boxes was supposed by them
to encase bibles, medicines, surgical instruments, antitoxins,
soaps, mosquito nets, photographs of American cities, and
of the Board of Foreign Missions that fathered my self-
sacrifice, a few volumes of Shakespeare and Browning, and
proper clothing for Christian heathen, of course more in
the nature of samples from the religious firms than of complete outfits for the whole tribe. The trusty packing-cases
in reality concealed every describable novelty of trinket,
gewgaw and bead, all the garish wonders of bizarre invention, and a quite incomparable selection of peculiar fire-
crackers and candies. There were ten of these chests, each
with a marvelous treasure peculiarly its own, but number
ten had one difference from the others, hereafter to be described—it was the pivot of my plan, the conception in
which my genius burst into full-orbed radiance. All were
lined with rubber to defend them against rain and damp.
Finally, one receptacle bore my private traps, an evening
suit vowed to planetary culture, a few books on which I
specially doted, including Plato, St. Augustine, Whitman,

Thomas a Kempis, Zola, Emerson, Ibsen, Tolstoy, Haeckel, Milton, Nietzsche, and a handful of conscientious modern radicals not so well known, for these sustain the soul to great enterprises—I am a true child of our ideal American Republic and absorb everything without believing much of anything—firearms, a diamond ring, my silk hat and over-alls.

CHAPTER II

The Rinyos

Having reached the borderland of the Rinyo state with aboriginal attendants collected in transit, I dismissed them all with generous benedictions and made my journey forward alone, instructing them to return for me in a year to receive their pay, which they tearfully consented to do. The poor fellows indeed exhibited signs of the deepest sorrow, never expecting to see me alive or dead again. I entered the enemies' country in the night and after traveling some distance toward the seat of the King, began the execution of my plan. I buried one of the chests with marks to indicate its hiding-place; and so proceeded, always by night, making a circuit of the royal village and from time to time interring another box. By day I recruited and slept, keeping my animals out of sight in dense groves. I was grateful to have the long journey over, for the size and weight of the chests had obliged the strapping of three animals together to sustain each burden. The heavy boxes lying across their backs and the disruption of their ordinary habits—for they were not broken to move in triplets—often chafed them and caused a panic, to my great apprehension, especially when there was no moon. Besides, a number of the mountain paths on which I ventured were intended for only one beast and it required great ingenuity and intrepidity on my part to guide them three abreast to the number of over thirty. When all the boxes were dispersed under the sod I therefore cheerfully turned the animals loose, with the precaution of secreting their trappings in a covered crevice of rock, and advanced toward the ruler's village with only the one that bore my personal comforts and professional articles.

I was received with gratifying cordiality and enthusiasm, but was at once cast into prison, which on reflection I considered a good sign; for they might have torn me limb from limb, or sportively thrown me from a high rock, or transfixed me with the evening spit; but their leniency for the time prevailed. I had not been long immured before I was of the opinion that their prison system needed reforming. It was quite too simple and ascetic to suit the expansive standards of modern life of even the criminal, still less of the cultivated missionary. They placed me against a rock and heaped fragments of granite against my surface until only my head was visible, nor did they even set a covering of any sort above me for protection against the torrid blaze of the sun. How they expected me to eat in this situation unless they fed me I have never been able to imagine, and the boulders pressed against my thorax with such acrimony that I doubt if I could have swallowed unaided. They seemed to be making ready to cast their javelins at my head for target practice, having, I suppose they imagined, amply protected my important parts.

In this awkward posture of affairs I signified my desire to see their King, a privilege which, being graciously accorded, led me into new difficulties. I informed his majesty, as well as I could with motions of the head and face, and expressive sounds, that I possessed secrets that would make him the most dreadful of living monarchs, thereby ardently inflaming his ambition and causing him to listen

willingly to sanitary overtures to enlarge my quarters and
give me facilities for expeditiously learning his language.
He appointed his Family Poet, the Chief Prophet of their
Idols, and the head of their Medical Faculty, who, by royal
decree were considered at that time the greatest intellects
of the realm, my instructors, promising that none of the
citizens should devour me except under such penalties as
made my existence for the time moderately secure.

I was taken out of my cage and presented with a domicile
hewn by nature in the rock, containing a very low entrance
which obliged me to creep in and out on my hands and
knees, and against which an enormous bulk of granite was
rolled by four huge savages when I was within. The King
informed me by signs that this precaution was taken as
much to preserve me from accidents incident to strangers
in their midst, as to prevent my escape. Twice a day the
stone was pushed aside so that I might promenade in public
with my four guards, and I confess I felt much safer at
home than abroad. Goaded by the fear that some native's
appetite might outrun his theories of happiness, I spent all
my time talking to one or other of my preceptors, even con-
straining the Chief of Idols to go upon my walks with me,
and thus I made such prodigious headway in grammar that
the King conceived me to be a great wit and proposed to
make me his court fool. Then, as often thereafter, I was
obliged to decline honors that were thrust upon me un-
sought, for it transpired that their rule was to kill most of
those whom they turned out of office to make room for
another. They had found that, having held office, a man
was never happy till he had eeled into another, that he was
never after at ease with his fellow savages, but kept himself apart from them with a contemptuous and often murderous disposition, and that the anxiety of the populace to
get a place was so strenuous that some became mad. And
they had discovered that killing the retired officials not only

made them happier but to some extent mollified the national
fever of others to succeed them.   In one or two instances
there proved to be a singularly fruitful exception to this
sanguinary maxim.

The King was not offended by my refusal to serve offi-
cially as his fool.   If anything he was rather more drawn
to me by my abnegation, considering me a gap in the continuity of nature as he had experienced it.   He said as
much in his childlike way.   I think this was the origin of
his suspecting me to be a god, a harmless fancy which I
encouraged.   From this moment, at least, dated our uncommon affection.   He would sit on my rock for hours together teaching me language, while I lay on my back inside
my den, for I could not sit upright.   He was a man of
exceeding sternness of character toward his wives and enemies, but trusting and devoted as a camel to those who won
his confidence.

As soon as I could trust my powers of speech in the ver-
nacular I carried out an important and daring design that
had formed in my brain.   I invited His Highness to conduct me to the most solemn place in his dominion, saying
that I had weighty matters on which to converse with him
in the deepest privacy.   Thereupon at his orders a huge
leathern gong was rung in the central part of the metropolis,
which caused all the inhabitants to gather about two trees
of colossal hight, connected near their tops by what appeared from the distance of the earth to be a rope.   I had
often noticed the natives display a curious ceremony at the
foot of these monstrous growths, for which I could divine
no natural reason.   At the base of each and circling it was
a trench two feet wide and equally deep, filled with ordinary
dust.   Into this once each day every inhabitant plunged his
head down to the shoulders and held it there vertically for
some time, with the dust gathered about him so that nothing
of his head or neck was visible.   When he could no longer

endure the situation, dirty, pallid, snorting and nearly dead for want of breath, he emerged. This, I subsequently learned, was one of their profoundest religious ceremonies. It was an act of spiritual purification secured through intimate veneration of the sacred trees. The dust was never changed, since its potency was believed to increase with the number of purifications accomplished in it.

This dust, as I later learned, was symbolic of ashes, which they thought to be man's spirit, because ashes remained when the body was burned. They imagined these ashes to be all-powerful, and always carried those of their ancestors in a bag about their necks; and a pinch of them was their chief medicine when sick. They kept the ashes of their divers forbears separate in little bags, and when they needed the virtue that had distinguished one of the dead they selected it from the appropriate ash bag—as when one was about to make a speech he swallowed a few grains of some departed orator in his family. When a man had consumed all the ashes of his deceased kin, it had been formerly the rule for him to offer himself for death as being drained of virtue, but this practice happily gave place to using dust symbolically as they advanced in enlightenment. The King had granted a monopoly of dust to the masters of the idols, who magically converted the dust into the ashes or spirits of the deceased as desired, and sold them to the people for a great revenue.

The connection of trees with this remarkable rite was at first obscure, but I learned that as trees grew out of dust and were reduced to ashes by fire, they seemed to the native to doubly possess the essence of men. It was believed that all whose bones were not burned entered into the trees and were concealed there, wherefore they worshipped the large trees as containing the greatest number of their friends. The growth of trees, according to them, was due to the death of human beings, so that when they wished their trees to grow they went out and slew some of the neighboring tribes. The bones of the slain were left unburned. They were more enlightened than I expected to find them on one point, for they regarded all the dead as equally friendly to them, whether of their own people or of a hostile race. A very important reason came later to light why these warlike excursions were necessarily very frequent and pious, constituting in fact the first principle of their religion. As some of the tribes thereabouts believed neither in dust nor ashes and even had an atheistical leaning toward water, it appeared to the Rinyos that the surest way to convert them was to burn the members of a few of their prominent families. But the common multitude of the conquered were not given to the fire after their slaughter; their flesh was stripped off and dried, which then made the regular staple of the Rinyo eating while it lasted. And as often as the food became precarious, so often was there a revival of religion among the Rinyos, and they went out to spread it among their neighbors.

CHAPTER III

King Milto

When the people were assembled the King led me to the slimmer of the two trees. It was of such girth that my arms, being extended to embrace it, were almost straight. Pointing upward he explained that we were to ascend and transfer ourselves, hanging by our hands, across the vine rope to the second tree, in whose soaring branches I perceived a curious basin-shaped structure resembling a huge umbrella opened with the concave upwards about the trunk.

"There," beamed the King, "is the sacred spot you desire to visit."

As I gazed limply into the air he graciously remarked that

none but warriors in whose royal arteries flowed the divine blood of many kings had ever succeeded in making the ascension. I saw that I must follow him aloft tranquilly or grace the public sideboard of the nation that evening, and I signaled him to lead on, designing to notice how he did it and snatch a second for meditation. He mounted with evident struggle in spite of his wealth of massive steel-knit sinews. When he was about half way up I called out that he had neglected a matter of vital moment and requested him to descend for its kingly consideration. Upon his doing so I discreetly intimated that it was unbecoming in a person of his quality to betray the preposterous strain he had exhibited before the jealous eyes of his people, and desired him to command the inhabitants to prostrate themselves with their faces in the earth. Being impressed by my words and having issued the order he mounted again, but with greatly abated vigor. When he had arrived at nearly the previous altitude I once more hailed him, announcing that I had forgotten some necessary elements of our conference which must be carried to the sacred fane. Having redescended, by this time badly winded and heaving violently, I told him that I should need two stones of certain dimensions for the lucid communication of my thought, and while he puffed I sought out two rocks of great solidity weighing about fifty pounds each, for the purpose of binding them about us for transit to the umbrageous shrine. Wilted and dripping with sweat as he was, he looked ruefully at the heavy mass I appointed to him, but submitted meekly while I fastened it in a large skin to his back, and accepted my orders to clamber first.

After gaining the lofty observatory he was to throw down the pelt for my use.

The poor monarch began the task once more, but, from fatigue and the ponderous weight swung on his neck, was this time unable to rise more than a quarter of the journey, when he came slipping back scarlet with shame, confusion and rage over his weakness. It was well for him that the tribe could not witness his humiliation or they might have resented his failure as a manifest exhaustion of kingly abilities and clamored for a competent chief. I rather regretted that I had plunged their noses into the public domain, for they might have elected me king. But one cannot foresee everything when trembling under death's auction hammer. And what if, after the vote, they had demanded a fulfilment of my election pledges by calling upon me to prove my kingly powers by achieving this very spectacular climb? Where every citizen is worth his weight in melenite it is best to tread softly and aspire lowly. If I am to practise tyranny I object to so many explosives in my worshippers. I rather they would have more clay and less enterprise in their composition, and I would sooner any day be the absolute president of ninety million civilized lead men than run a unanimous despotism over nine thousand cases of primitive hysteria. It calls for a supreme hysteric to govern this field of originality, and only a supreme dimension of human lead in the other. I concluded to let Milto reign a while longer. He seemed convinced that it would be an artless frolic for me to accomplish the feat that had balked him, whence his respect for me expanded amazingly. Calling him a girl and displaying such pity and contempt as the occasion demanded to invigorate his awe of my attributes, I informed him that the next less sacred place he had would do for our meeting, provided it was on the ground. This he interpreted as a further scathing rebuke and he led the way, with head hanging, to a grotto in the mountain side, leaving the community forgotten, flat on their bellies and foreheads. The spacious cavern to which he brought me contained an aggregation of seats of sundry shapes, nicely constructed of human bones; and on one of these pleasant memories my companion hospitably motioned me to sit, which I did with a certain tinge of loathing. I then declared my message, beginning with these words as nearly as I can remember:

"Oh, King, awful depository of posthumous astonishments," for I was a devout evolutionist. I then explained that I was the ambassador from a new deity named Buzzrack, to reveal gifts that this god had secreted in various places in the Rinyo territory, one of which was to be brought to light every moon with the assistance of the two stones. I found that these articles operated forcibly on the great potentate's superstition. In return for the celestial presents, upon whose wonders I expatiated glowingly, I informed His Majesty that Buzzrack desired some yellow sand that was scattered about his domain, and which at the end of twelve moons I was to carry home to the god.

King Milto listened rapturously to these allurements, as I had expected he would, promising volubly to convert all his people to this generous divinity and entreating me to bring forth the first treasure without loss of time.

"There is one matter I had nearly forgotten," said I speaking of course in his language. "If anything should happen to me while I am in your midst you will lose these wonderful presents, because I alone know where they are. The wrath of Buzzrack will give your tribe no peace afterwards and he will cause you to be exterminated by your enemies."

I know not whether the great Milto was more agitated by cupidity or by his pious fears, but he instantly promulgated the decrees I desired. He went so far as to proclaim that I was a blood relation of the god I represented, or his private secretary, or some fearful functionary or other from the clouds. He declared that if any brother did me the slightest harm his whole family should be baked alive for a public breakfast and the perpetrator himself reduced to a vegetarian for one year before death, a penalty most dreaded by these pampered pagans. Feeling now reasonably secure I notified the terrible monarch that on the morrow the first box of riches would be revealed.

The King immediately dispatched numerous heralds to summon his people from all parts, and at ten in the morning his whole tribe, having assembled, set forth in grand procession. Two superb young giants, bearing the stones that had saved my life the day before, marched in front under my directions toward the corner of the empire where I had made the first interment. From time to time with great ceremony I ordered them to deposit the stones on the ground a little distance apart and placing my head between them so that one ear rested against each, listened for some minutes with an impressive display of awe. I was pleased to observe that this solemn maneuver had the effect of convincing them of the truth of the new religion I intended them to espouse.

At length I brought the multitude to a halt and announced that we were within the sacred circle where my deity had concealed the treasure, and that only myself, the King and the three great men already mentioned might approach the holiest ground without certain death. The five of us advanced, I bearing a peculiar rod in my hand as a conductor of magic. "Dig," I articulated in cavernous liturgical tones at the right place, taking my seat in a commanding posture upon the sacred stones. They did so trembling and the great box was soon uncovered, to the unspeakable exultation of their four dignities, who projected themselves about it in a series of dances and contortions wonderful and terrifying to see. Their excitement became so violent that I was in mortal terror lest they should utterly lose their self-control and attack me in the exuberance of their religious ecstasy, but it appears that this is their usual manner of showing devotion to whatever they like and that they forget it all the next minute.

When the frenzy had subsided—and in a twinkling no
traces of it were left, so that I doubted if I had not been
the subject of an optical illusion—they drew the precious
article out of the earth and deposited the sacred stones on
the spot where it had lain, upon which at the bottom of the
hole I stood for a few minutes with my arms stretched into
the air and an indescribable expression upon my face. Then
I ordered them to shout at the top of their lungs that the
deity might hear, and afterwards to lift out the precious
stones and fill up the hole. They raised the box on their
shoulders, though from the effects of their prostrating im-
patience hardly able to carry it, and returned to the multitude. I requested King Milto to cause a stentorian cry to
issue from the entire congregation, to rend space and notify
the god that the gift was received and appreciated, since
their four voices might not have penetrated the eternal
mind. After this declaration of gratitude the opulent bulk
was shouldered by ten colossi and the whole nation headed
for its capital.

In the vast public field, where on great occasions the entire tribe congregated, the festival of opening the box was
now begun. I had fastened on the lid firmly with screws,
intending to preserve the packing-case for deporting gold,
and producing a screw-driver I soon had the cover off. The
behavior of all the leading men of the commonwealth at
this point fascinated my attention. Their greed for the
screws was so keen and their conduct so turbulent that I
was forced to appeal to the majesty of the throne to re-
strain them from secreting these necessary articles about
their persons. Even the King was burying the screw-driver
in his hair when I ordered him to desist, assuring him that
he should have no more supernal delicacies if he dared to
rob me.

It would require a genius of Homeric brilliance and Dan-
tean accuracy to depict the hideous scene which now enacted

itself, and as the ancient delineators of greed and ghastliness
are dead I will leave it to your imaginations to intensify
every sentence that I now utter, with befitting emotions of
horror. When I drew forth the first glass necklace and held
it above my head to the astonished gaze of all, the people
were wrought up into a bellowing excitement more like a
raging tempest at sea viewed from an oarless skiff than anything else I have experienced. They roared and foamed,
they swayed back and forth like a lofty edifice about to fall
before a hurricane; all the passions of the infernal world
screamed through their dazzling savage teeth, bursting
forth in outrageous inhuman sounds which seethed, sput-
tered and exploded with a ponderous din, furiously batter-
ing the shrinking ear with their horrible hectoring clangor.
In my judgment, at the time, all the gold in Africa would
not compensate a man for gazing five seconds into that
awful human abyss. I never again could believe that my
fellowmen were anything but exaggerated apes.

The scene had the curious effect of touching my religious
susceptibilities. I asked myself what I could do to elevate
such persons morally, wishing to leave them better than I
had found them, to sow some seeds of spiritual good in
their shaly souls. It must not surprise you that my religious emotions flourished luxuriantly in their proper
sphere of my nature, removed from the chilling realities of
the world. Yet how was it possible to implant a sense of
the true God in the sordid jelly of avarice composing this
nation? Just picture it! A handful of gaudy glass made
them fiends! Dignity, decorum, patriotism, morality,
religion, family affection, were all alas chased helter-skelter
out of their immortal souls by a miserable string of yellow
shams. If the beads had cost something I could have understood it. I was justified in despairing of their virtue
and I doubted if civilization or prayer could soften such
cupidity. Perhaps if I could have shown them something

of real value, a dollar in gold or an American lady's ideals, they would have relapsed into pure impersonal protoplasm, which if you think of it is nothing but unorganized greed, but I had taken care to bring nothing so incendiary with me.

These reflections came in their full force later. At that vivid moment I was cursing the lot of a missionary with my whole theology and preparing to die. I renounced riches and swore to live a consecrated life in the slums of a city if my life was spared. I vowed to God I would spend my days in reasoning affectionately with the rich on the sin of luxury and foible of robbing the poor, whenever they did me the honor to invite me to their homes. Yet I felt reconciled to my Creator, and deliriously prepared for an immediate encounter with Him if that was to be my fate. In short I was rather beside myself, as the bravest man might be in such a mess, standing there the lust and goal of forty thousand wild beasts. I don't know exactly what I did, I yelled, that I remember, from infection, I suppose, not fear, and stamped, and contrived by unconscious cerebration and writhing to tear every garment on me more or less, and then, in a wild frenzy of cowardice, leaped upon the shoulders of the King to get away from the lunatic mob, where I clasped my two hands, still holding the abominable trinket, into His Highness' hair for balance and steadying—and that unprecedented, unpremeditated, reflex, hysterical act saved the dynasty and me. For the fools thought I was crowning their King with some new and exalted ceremony from the celestials who had made me their ambassador, the tempest of their savage cupidity was for a moment lulled, and that instant restored the wits of the King. He was now equal to the emergency. With me still on his head, forgotten, he tore up and down the crowd like a Medusa, an absolute madman, knocking down whatever came in his way, whether giants or girls, so that in a twinkling all the inhabitants of the kingdom, in a panic of

fright, were fleeing toward the horizon while he drove and
beat them much as a bull tosses lambs. Having quieted
the tribe, His Highness' wrath subsided as suddenly as it
had flamed up. As we strolled back to the box he frequently
struck his regal chest in exultation, giving forth a deafening snort.

"It is the only way to keep order in a kingdom of ac-
cursed dogs and blighted heathen," he blustered. "Cloven
heads are a specific for cloven hoofs. My children are a
people with rancorous passions and venomous aspirations;
all of them want everything they see; they're a bilious
crew, devoid of reason or generosity; avarice is their
crowning emotion and murder their pastime. I have a
higher religion, but it is too pure for them. I try to
teach them unselfishness by taking the best of everything
for myself, that they may learn not to covet. But the swine
are not spiritual and they can't understand. I don't think
they'd recognize their own spirits if they met them on the
street. Ingratitude consumes them and they despise education. I sometimes think I'll resign and live quietly the
rest of my days on a pension in an oasis, leaving them to
tear each other's bowels out in peace. Brute force alone
sanctifies them, nothing else, and thank God I have that
gift of grace, also."

"You ought to thank me and God for saving you this
time," exclaimed I with considerable heat, "for I saw how
it was going and jumped on your head purposely to suppress the riot. I pity your brute force if I hadn't done so.
Religion and reason are above brute force always, or were
this time at any rate. The herd recognize superior beings
instinctively when they are on top."

To this he answered nothing, but continued to heave out
his breast and beat it.

CHAPTER IV

The Treasure Is Divided

To be beforehand of another insurrection when the next beads appeared, Milto ordered the population to form in concentric circles about us and to stand on one leg. Whoever disobeyed this rescript even for the fraction of a second was to lose his share of the gifts. Statecraft thus prevailed, reminding me of the ways of the cunning rulers of enlightened republics. Humility now fawned upon the heels of diabolical disobedience, and the multitude became like fawns, their will engulfed in the majestic conceit of one genius. When they could no longer endure the strain upon one leg they hopped into the air and came down on the other. The King meanwhile sent his body guard through the ranks to spy out the fractious. He kept his subjects in this attitude before rescinding his order until they were reduced to such exhaustion that they could hardly stand, still less sulk, but so intense was the ardor of all for the lovely wonders in waiting that none of them yielded to the temptation to rest on both feet or sit down, not even the women or children. Upon my hinting surprise at this in a low tone at the ear of Royalty, he answered whispering that all of them would sooner die than show the white feather in this ordeal; that it was in fact one of their great periodic examinations of character and knowledge, which those aspiring to respect, as well as those pining for office either about his person or that of the idols, were obliged to frequently endure. Those who failed were lost, for they died of shame if they were not taken off secretly by their peers before they had time to do so. Their system of education rested on these examinations, which incited them to perseverance. There was no part of their educational scheme that equally encouraged the higher qualities.

While the nation was thus improving itself, the King called his select advisers about him, all of whom were men of such advanced age that they were unable to stand upright, but were obliged to creep. It was one of the excellent customs of the tribe to reverence these helpless ancients, whose minds were even more decayed than their bodies, as superior beings, and implicitly to obey whatever the Crown decreed after counselling with them. I was much edified by their aspect. Several were stone blind, others stone deaf, still others so stricken with paralysis of the brain that they could remember not more than two words of their language and were obliged to repeat these over monotonously to express such ideas as they had, of course conveying no meaning or sense to anyone. I counted the number of times that one of them in a speech repeated the word meaning in their language money, and found it to be nine hundred and forty. This was the only syllable the poor old fellow could recall. In truth among the whole lot of these monuments of antiquity, some of whom were at least two hundred years old, owing to the salubriousness of the climate, the simplicity of their later years, and a peculiar article of diet, none that I could perceive had more than one of his original five senses left and quite a number were not even so gifted as to have retained one.

This grave assemblage now went into solemn counsel with the King as to the just disposition of the contents of the box, as they lay spread about in full view. The will and wisdom of the tribe were supposed to express themselves through these experienced patriarchs. He who proved to be the most eloquent orator rose upon his hands and knees from the reclining posture and delivered the remarkable address to which I have already referred out of the word money. He was listened to with profound silence and respect by all who could hear. His speech ended only when he sank into a complete swoon lasting an hour, which in that tribe passed for divine approbation of the sentiments uttered. Nor was anything done to restore the weary sage to animation, for he was supposed to be holding a secluded and intimate communion with the gods. He was followed by one who could neither see, hear, feel nor utter a sound, but who, in a sitting position propped against a stump, beat the earth in front of him most vindictively with a stick for some time. All those in whose memory survived the words necessary to do so then gave an account of their younger days, which had made the sitting interminable had they not all spoken at once, most of them supposing they were the only ones addressing the meeting. While this transpired a venerable statesman, shrunken till in many places the bones had worked out of their skinny sheath and economical nature had withdrawn the kindly cuticle of which they had no further need, but crowned with a reverend head several spaces larger than those of our greatest civilized governors and savants, which gave him an aspect of intellectual grandeur quite startling and horrible, although powerless to lift this monstrous cranium from the soil, crawled forward feet foremost dragging his head behind to the seat of His Majesty and there scrawled in the earth the extraordinary figures meaning "sons," "sons-in-law," "grandsons," "great-grandsons," "nephews," all with very large heads, which, by the supplicating motions of his gums and eyelids, occurring in rhythm, was plainly a request for these individuals to be rewarded by the King suitably to their scintillating merits. The faculties of the rest of the Senate being past use they had now all been heard from and the King arose.

"These sages have decided," said he, "that as father and representative of my people I shall receive half of the loving god's gift. The half that I take is really a gift to yourselves, since as head of the State I am your personification and essence. I will not thank you for what you present to yourselves."

"Yes! Yes! " cried such of the old chancellors as were able to speak, and the orator called out "Money."

"Very good," said the King, "then it is a vote."

He proceeded to select everything that according to his taste was the handsomest of the lot, until he had far exceeded the half. His people being now sufficiently worn out and subdued from standing on one leg, were permitted to resume a natural posture, whereon most of them collapsed at full length upon the ground in utter prostration. He then repeated in a loud voice that he had obeyed the commands of the old men concerning the divine gift, to which they all assented with acclamatory salvos.

Turning brazenly to me he requested me to swear an oath that such had been the heavenly giver's commands, and to test the rascal's impudence I replied that he like all truly sublime potentates and politicians was able to read and do the will of Heaven by perusing his own self-interest. It astonished me that such craven popular docility followed upon the people's tempestuous graspingness of a little while before. It seemed a case of despotism conducted by assassination *from* the throne—a very antique state of darkness, which had been altered in later countries to assassination of the throne. Being a born conservative, it is better, said I to myself, that half a nation should die of assassination conducted by the ruler and his satellites, than that one king or rich man should perish to save them, and in no country do a score million of citizens equal in value one king or plutocrat.

Shaking off these reflections I edged up to the Royal Grandeur to ask him the meaning of his behavior.

"Why," he explained, "if these brilliants were passed around to everybody they would make no show and the people would not feel grand, rich, proud, sublime, luxurious and pampered; but if I take the best and keep them in one mass as my own, to enjoy them on myself, they create a magnificent display, every poor devil in the tribe feels that he owns them personally through me, because I am *his* monarch, he struts and purrs like a true slave when he sees me wearing them, and learns to feel as if they were on him, who never owned the picture of a jewel's shadow; his mind gives him more bright palpitations than all these realities distributed could, though he would then have his proper share; he is happier than a bird all wings or a Rinyo all stomach; he is not jealous of the glories that beautify his Prince, but would perish of grief, or slaughter his peers from malice if one of them had two beads to his one. In a word, I benevolently take these things to save my beloved children from themselves. I am a moderator between their hates, which is the true function of a great and magnanimous sovereign who is above earthly passions and foibles; I arbitrate between their little furies, their trivial bedlams, their creature avarices, their carnal animosities, their factional eruptions, their truculent rebellions; I let them wear out their deadly propensities on each other, and step in at the funeral of the fiercest with kindly compromises in time to deter the survivors from renewing the combat and destroying the Fabric of State. I am interested in that fabric above everything and am placed here on earth to preserve it. They must have something to fight, and if they did not have one another they would fight me, than which for the welfare of Africa I would rather anything else should happen and that all my subjects should perish. A country without a people may survive, but one without a State has but a short time to live. Government is deeply interested in everything which, even through the medium of some temporary uneasiness like the slaughter of the population, may tend finally to compose the minds of the subjects and to conciliate their affections.

"I also perform the function of sitting like a heavenly orb in their sky and radiating ideas of goodness, self-sacrifice, mercy and contempt of all things vile and mercenary into them, ideals which could never germinate spontaneously in the flinty plasm of their sodden souls. For them I am Goodness, Justice, Power, Poison, Punishment and Love, compounded into one human form, which they must see with their eyes of flesh for inspiration, and I don't know what would become of their morals if they hadn't me for an example."

Before completing his remarks he paused to finish adjusting the tinsel ornaments upon his glistening ebony frame, a work in which he had been ardently engaged while speaking. He drew necklace after necklace over his sceptred head, until his great neck was encircled with a volume of beaded glass more than a foot thick, reaching out from his ears toward his distant shoulder-tips; the leglets and anklets he strung on so thick and effectively from hip to heel that he looked as if he were clad in a pair of dense brass trousers, while he made his bracelets rattle clear up to the armpits; the earrings which were of all lengths from one to ten inches he fastened to his waistband and I showed him how to connect the breast-pins to these short clothes; for the attachment of tin crowns his crisp voluminously tufted hair gave excellent space, so that without crowding he fastened on nine of them, obtaining something of the venerable aspect which our best sculptors have imparted to the head of Jove; and having scrutinized himself for some time with no feigned or temperate admiration in a looking-glass from the box, the first arrival of reflection in that part of the world, and tantalizingly postured on the foppish eminence of the backs of four Rinyos whom he made to kneel under him, he took up his cogitations where he had left them and said:

"The ideas I have been giving you are the judgment of

my old men, arrived at in grand conclave after a sleep of thirty-six hours; I applied the vote without waking them up and they were unanimous. Their opinion is known to be the will of Heaven, and if any person makes light of that he becomes an outcast and forfeits the protection of our tribe; we express the situation by calling him a wild beast, for it is the duty and privilege of whoever can catch him to eat him. It is a long time since the edict of the aged was questioned by a heretic, as long ago as my Grandfather's death and my Father's coronation, when a seditious faction of the tribe refused to recognize the former as dead, albeit the old men had pronounced him so in spite of his arguments to the contrary. My Grandfather then sided with the inflammatory mob and declared himself alive, a great mistake of his because it countenanced lawlessness, for when the law said he was dead, he was dead, but Father upheld the righteous authority of the primeval patriarchs, taking his stand on the incontestable principle that if their decree was doubted once there would never again be an infallible supreme court. They took up arms and fought for some years, and Grandfather fell by Father's hand, and thus ended his dangerous attempt to establish an impious and unruly innovation. When the Ancients now say that a person is dead he is the first to agree with them. About the glorious holiday and festive hunt we have for him when some gay prattling youth questions the utterance of these immortal sages, I was going to say—but I'll tell you the rest some other time."

He broke off because of what I shall now relate.

CHAPTER V

A MAGNIFICENT CARNAGE

About two-fifths of the articles remained to be divided, whose disposition interested me deeply. Casting my eyes around I saw a group of about forty men standing apart in a prominent place and displaying much more eagerness and expectancy than the rest. Having by this time become somewhat adept in the internal characteristics of the population I quickly recognized this body as the foremost personages of the realm, after the King himself. There were the Chief Priest of the Idols and the Chief Medicine Man, another functionary was the Preserver of Bones, while a fourth was already known to me as the High Polisher of Skulls; the two principal Cooks to His Majesty were also present, one being Cook Extraordinary of Foreigners, the other of Home Products, for various culinary arts were applied to the preparation of their own species which were not accorded to remains of strange extraction. A singular peculiarity of their cooking was their performance of it without the aid of fire, to their stomachs a most economical and palatable omission.

About ten of the group were high dignitaries of this kind, of one other of whom I must not omit special mention, the most consequential and influential of all, he being called the Servant of the King's Feet. His function was to wash these extremities of his royal master, which he did by licking them over with his tongue, water being regarded by this tribe as unholy. He had been appointed to this dignity because of the enormous fluency of his tongue, which made the operation very speedy, and this liquid oratory was the chief symptom of statesmanship and title to power in that liberal democracy. Next to him in place and authority stood one who was called the King's Ear, because he was expected to hear and convey to His Sovereignty whatever desires or dangerous discontents the people entertained. This man, who was a most trusted adviser to the King, was required to transact his business with great punctuality. Every night after the King had fallen asleep he was to relate the desires of the people, while the dangerous discontents if he heard of any were to be conveyed at once to the Domestic Cook, who gave immediate attention to the disorder by serving up the dissatisfied to the King at his next meal. Thus a marvelous degree of internal contentment was preserved by this great leader of men, with little visible friction to the realm and no carking disturbance of his own peace.

Besides the ten most high officials there were thirty in the company who were called Guardians of the Food. One was overlord of each species of animal hunted, raised, or trapped by the nation, including foreign and domestic human flesh, and one presided over each family of vegetables and herbs on which they fed. These celebrated men were the safety-valves or balance-wheels of the food supply, keeping the market steady. When a citizen brought home game from the hunt or killed a domestic fowl he was obliged to carry it first to the guardian of its species for judgment defining the portion of the carcass the slayer was entitled to retain without endangering the public equilibrium. Likewise if a citizen dug a root out of the earth he must convey it to its guardian for an honest division. The custom was for the guardian to allow not less than one-tenth of a beast to its catcher, altho precedent was here loose and elastic, and he might be made to do with a twentieth and was sometimes compelled to go and catch a second beast for the privilege of having caught the first, and deliver them both;—the amount varied with a mass of circumstances and considerations which the guardians had in their memory and the rest could not pry into without crime.

If they questioned the acts of the guardians they were hanged as anarchists. The nine-tenths, or whatever the great economic law of the guardian's appetite specified, that dignitary retained for his own family and his favorites.

The arrangement had been infinitely satisfying to everybody: the tribesmen were kept in a perpetual motion productive of soothing prostration, as constrained to be ten times more active in order to live, while the great, likewise enjoying ten times more food than they would naturally have had except for this wise convention, were enabled to be ten times greater. Their splendor also co-operated with that of the King to dilate the feeling of reflected personal magnificence in the most despicable and needy.

Such was the constitution of the collection of men who were holding themselves apart from the rest with a bearing of uncommon poise and grandeur. The King convoked his decrepit philosophers a second time, which consisted of sending his pages around to wake them by rapping their heads with a stick, and without going through the previous preliminary of stating the matter to them he announced their conclusion as follows:

"It is the divination of this most honorable congress on earth that the bountiful giver of these gifts intended our great men to receive half of what remains, that the dignity and glory of the kingdom may be upheld and the sublime services of the great to the common people partially recompensed."

The pages, who were doing their best to keep the ancients awake by pounding them on the head with thin sticks anointed by the King for that use, and succeeding very badly, themselves cried "yes" to this decree of the King's, but their words were hardly audible, for the forty illustrions gentlemen did not await the capping of the ceremony but rushed forward in fierce confusion, tearing, scratching and kicking right and left as they ran, each trying to strike his neighbor or trip him down, and succeeding so well that in a moment the entire band of eminent social lights was piled up in a ferocious howling heap, reminding one of a foot-ball rout conducted by professional prize fighters intensified and complicated by college culture. They writhed indeed like a mass of huge passionate snakes in fiery death agony, from which I thought none could emerge with enough of himself in one place to make life worth living.

I confess that I tingled slightly at this spectacle, and looked askance at the Many-Crowned King expecting him to interfere to save the lives of his sweetest subjects, but to my consternation he was gazing on the gory scene with stolid placidity, engorging the dripping tragedy, as it seemed, with the voluptuous urbanity of an insatiable connoisseur. A sense of his greatness impregnated me as I stared at him. He had the right stuff in him for a clergyman or a convict. He was a jocular high priest of this bloody gladiatorial world; and he could tolerate brutality, the first attribute of pure culture. His sympathy extended to all, to the murdered as well as to the murderers, so that he was modern and scientifically chic to the bone. He would have made a respectable president if our professors could have had him to file off the edge of his shrieks, wash him and round him out. Even without their scrubbing he shone like a bright placid lonesome frozen star in the lifted infinite remoteness of indifference. He had the learned man's broad liberality to deeply venerate Whatever Is, and to spend his whole power venerating it. We need more such. The forty thousand American professors are too few for the work. They cannot venerate as much as Whatever Is deserves. More are needed to venerate Decay at its full worth.

But I am merely human; I have the sensibilities of my kind. I am not built to observe forty men butchering one another in a heat over no higher object than a few paltry trinkets, without some feeling, besides the religion I have in me, and I was moved by humanity to expostulate with the stony ruler.

"It will be a great loss to your realm if those lordly luminaries die?" I suggested with a rising inflection of the voice, in order not to seem impudent. "Could you find any to take their places? Genius is rare, talent painful to mould, considerable economic outlay is required to raise up men to large affairs, African trade is slack, and money scarce."

I thought I would drive home the sharpest darts at once, and goad his sensibilities into action in time to redeem a few of his first people, but that only showed how little I yet knew of savage souls and civics. He simply looked queerer than I had ever seen him and pursed out his luxuriant lips a prodigious distance from his shimmering teeth while his eyes had the astounding effect of glaring and revolving in opposite directions violently.

"What are you doing with your lips?" I asked with dignity, for I will not bear everything even when I am in a minority.

"Praying," said he, "that the ones who ought to conquer may do so."

CHAPTER VI.

The Position of the King's Feet in the Fabric of State.

Then he relaxed and came and sat down on one corner of the box in a brotherly fashion, beckoning me to occupy ingly and conversed amiably, never taking his eyes off the another, while he threw his arm over my shoulder caress-ghastly encounter.

"Anybody in the nation could do what these men do,"
he said in a confidential tone, "but that is not generally
understood. For example the entire tribe suppose that
the licking of my feet is a very mysterious and difficult
business only to be learned with vast assiduity and whose
virtue lies in doing it a certain way, and for the matter of
that the washer of my feet believes so himself and plumes
himself as a most recondite and scarce phenomenon. But
indeed it makes no difference at all how it is done. The
intricacy was invented to muddle and awe the populace.
For that purpose the mazy art was slowly grown by my
forefathers through many glorious Kings. The feet are
mapped out into a multitude of spaces: the officer is required to lick a certain number of times in a certain direction on a certain part, then to alter the course until all
the varieties of liquefaction have been applied; for each
space has its peculiar set of directions and particular number of licks. I only remember a few of the laws myself,
such as the west quarter of the end of the little toe on the
right foot, which must be licked thirty and a half times
from side to side, while the end of the other little toe
receives forty-seven and a third strokes in the same field
up and down. There are several other very elaborate
passes on both of these sections which I do not recollect.
Each foot has a treatment in every respect diverse from
the other, whence the processes are excessively toilsome
to master. Of the right foot the licker is permitted to take
only the big toe completely into his mouth, whereas if he
should neglect to take in all five toes of the left, the penalty
is death. There is also a special punishment belonging to
every kind of failure in this office, although the death
sentence applies to several of them. Should he touch the
tip of his tongue to the wrong ankle his tongue is cut out."

"If you don't know the rules yourself how do you know
when he goes wrong?" I demanded. "It seems to me you
are likely to take an innocent life."

"We have a Trainer to inspect the Feet Washer," answered King Milto with much satisfaction, "and he stands by whenever the ceremony is performed. These two men are dreadful enemies, as well as their families to the distance of fifth cousins. The feud cuts into the very flesh of the tribe, and the principals think each other congenital imbeciles. I don't understand this for I can see no difference in them. When the trainer says the licker has blundered the licker denies it and denounces the trainer as a hopelessly corrupt noodle and knave. They compose the delicate dispute by fighting, when to the defeated one is administered the penalty. If neither whips I decide it any way that comes into my head and they think I'm infallible. If I say the great toe nail has been licked seventeen times to the right from the earliest antiquity, altho it was only seven times, they lawfully believe me against their own certainty."

"You must dispose of a good many leading citizens in the course of a lustrum."

"We generally average four 'King's Feet,' as we briefly call the washers, and the same number of trainers every moon. It is part of our living and it keeps down the population."

"I should think you would find it pretty hard to induce anyone to serve in the position," I exclaimed, grievously shocked.

The King laughed all over, causing the shell bracelets about his knees and elbows to jingle like sleighbells.

"Hook! Hook! Hook!" chucked His Majesty, when the convulsions of his system had abated, "every man and child in the kingdom is in training for it and would give his head just to hold the place one day so that it could be said in his family after he was dead that he had been officer of the feet. If I didn't hinder by making learning the rules of licking so prodigiously hard every grown person in the nation would come forward and beg for the honor, tho he knew he was to die for it in twenty-four hours. The country would be depopulated."

"They must be uncommon fools; how do you prevent it?"

"We make them learn the table of rules perfectly from beginning to end and backwards before they can apply; our examinations are days of inimitable pleasure on the crimson canvass of average existence here."

"Do you mean to say that everybody in the tribe is studying to learn how to lick your feet according to your ridiculous made-up system, which you admit amounts to nothing anyhow?" I sneered incredulously, quite forgetting the respect due his Illustrious Essence.

"Precisely; why not? You wouldn't have people grow up uneducated and idle would you?"

Stunned and staggered I could simply say that I had thought doing useless things the worst kind of idleness, and ask what he meant, which he blandly elucidated, with irrelevant flourishes of his fists in my vicinity with barbaric gusto.

"You see, the office of licking my feet being the highest within reach of my people, it is the just and lofty ambition of everyone, down even to the sewer-cleaners, bankers and tramps, to attain to it before he dies. Having arrived at this dizzy summit there is nothing left for him to long or live for, the goal is reached, his solid fame is immortal and secure. Nor does he gather brighter luster by holding it two months than by wearing it one day: the glory resides in the office, by no means in the period or conduct of any one therein. I make it so. Were I to announce that I had elevated my Flesh-Scraper (the lowest and most despised outcast in the realm, because he is relegated to the performance of the most useful service) into Grand Vizier of my Toes, and were then to kill him instantly, having

suffered him to apply his fleeting tongue to my pedal
extremities only once, he would be revered as highly, as
long remembered, and as passionately sung of as those
who have transacted the business a hundred times accurately
in the midst of domestic assassins and foreign complications,
and who have repeatedly rescued my Functions of State
from contamination.   It brings out a child's moral character to fix his eye early on great things, does it not?
I fix the nation's eyes on my Feet.   I think it is this certainty that anyone with a flowing tongue, polymorphous
memory, pickpocket's luck, and plush principles may lick
my feet sometime if he lives, that keeps alive the conscience
of the race and makes us spare the children of our conquered foes to grow up and be conquered and eaten later.
I don't allow any of them to hang on to the high place
longer than two moons.   The labor of licking is very trying to the weak, they grow slim and are ugly to look upon
afterwards; the strong wax so tough with the exercise
and ecstasy that they are not fit to eat and hence never
assimilate properly with their countrymen again; and all
get the feet-licking habit so firmly rooted that thenceforth
they go about in the street with their tongues out going
through the motions, and in fact licking everything they
come to, from the newspaper editors to the lampposts.   I
dislike this because it vulgarizes sacred things.

"One day, I may remark in confidence, would satisfy
the majority, for there is no pleasure in the office itself
I can tell you.   I get about half my fun out of those fellows.
While one is licking my heel I jab my toe into his eye or
knock his teeth down his throat according as I happen to
feel at the time; they never issue from their term of office
with any hair, for I take care to pull it out; you noticed
that a number of these antiquated members of my Cabinet
had no eyes in their sockets, I presume—well, I playfully
gouged them out.   The Council is entirely composed of

survivors of attendance on my feet, and those antediluvian relics are not all of them so ancient as they look. Do you see that gibbering dignitary who seems to be a hundred and ninety? He's only in his forty-seventh year, he was stalwart and hale when he ascended to the trust of Licking two years ago, in two months he was in about the condition you now see, and I retired him. I don't think he has aged much since, I'm very proud of him, I expect he'll keep a few years longer and look four hundred in his latter days. He is one of the wisest in the pack too, for he is completely mad. I go by his opinion when I daren't trust some of the livelier sparks."

"Is that what your education culminates in?" I asked with a fervid inclination to try the treatment of knocking him down.

"Oh, yes, I was telling you something about that, wasn't I? Well, in order to prevent them from being ready for the eminent station of licking all at the same time, which of course they are all fitted for by nature and predilection without study if I chose to divulge it, entrance thereinto is made famously complicated that it may take about thirty years to master its tangled singularities, and a man has to have a first-class mind to do it in that time. As this is the crowning glory of a human career and the aim universal in my realm, preparation for it makes men ready for every inferior duty in the tribe, so that we never have difficulty in selecting those best suited for our multifarious posts."

"Do you pick your chief cooks and head hunters and generals in that way?"

"Yes, and our guardians of the food also. We find those who have taken the longest course in the licking science to be superlatively prepared for all public service. Conscientious fidelity to the highest ideal is the parent of all kinds of aptitude. These gentlemen that you see there tumbling over and tearing one another up into morbid

anatomy are those who have mastered all the intricacies of
licking, taken the highest degree, you might say, and are
chafing for the present incumbent to die. Training in the
twelve thousand motions of the tongue and the twelve
thousand acts of memory, the accordant postures of the
neck, backbone and knees, and the versatile condition of
mind, has been found to shape a man for success in everything that has to be done in a commonwealth. You saw
a party of our young braves climbing after nuts the other
day: that is one of our skilled industries, and the climbers
are appointed on the same principle, only from the lower
grades, not yet having qualified in the advanced lubrications
and oratories of state-craft. They can climb trees which
the uneducated can't touch. Their backs are supple and
their knees twine around everywhere, while for hanging
on to whatever they get hold of they simply excel monkeys.
We find too that the constant use of the tongue is making
that member grow longer and more useful every year, and
we believe it is to become a sixth sense and a third arm
to supply the lack of the tail which man through some
accident has lost."

"By George!" cried I, "I had noticed how long the tongues
of your tribe are without suspecting the reason of it, and
I had mentally named you The Long-Tongues."

"Very good," answered Milto, pleased, "if you remain
with us a year you will see a still greater outcrop of that
instrument, and can supply a full report of the science of
Feet-Licking to your Master, which may enlighten him.
You have struck the keynote of our existence. We have
an ideal toward which we faithfully strive and when our
tongues are a foot long we shall begin to realize it: we
desire to live exactly as we please and to believe that we
are living entirely as we ought. Our philosophers by looking steadily at the heavens with their empty sockets have
made the prodigious discovery that the higher civilization

from certain inhabited stars passes from thence to us, and the pith of the great celestial doctrine they have caught and interpreted is that if men can believe right they *are* right, tho they do wrong. Mere doing is nothing, but feeling and believing are the whole matter. For instance, we have a moral prejudice against eating our mothers, but we find this fallacy is corrected by cultivating the opinion that we are not eating them when we are doing so. Nothing assists us to eradicate such errors more than a colleague with a great tongue standing in the hall during the meal and repeating rapidly and loudly while swinging his arms and making faces that we are not eating our mothers. After a few performances the new opinion is fixed and we can let him apply his tongue to the correction of our other faults. We sometimes stain the speaker's tongue black and paint his skin fiery red to convince the people that he is inspired,—a great aid to conscience and digestion, you can relish your parents a third more. Of course if the tongue were two or three feet long it would wield irresistible persuasion and a number of them swung in unison and falling upon the ears of the people would be excellent weapons of conviction. Incomparable invention! To achieve this mighty force all the energies of our tribe are centered in licking. In the sublime future every desire of our hearts will be satisfied through the perfection of this function, and we shall glory in our conquest of ignorance. If I should lose my feet and retard the practice of licking we should have some terribly dark ages."

He was radiant and I mused.

"All is clear, save one thing," I said. "I have no doubt the philosophers can see what goes on in the stars, but can they hear the orators?"

"Easily," Milto rejoined, with the motion of rolling up his bracelets for serious consideration. "They first break their ear-drums,—the stone deaf not needing to do so—

then they listen: being disembarrassed of outward confu-
sions the subtler impressions from the universe are regis-
tered within, they can plainly hear the stellar orators and
a great number of other infinite processes concealed from
common sense. They claim they can hear the Almighty
think, and why not if they first void their minds of all
feelings and thoughts? Our chief search aims to penetrate
the Almighty's thinking, and all our licking has no ultimate
purpose but understanding that. There is piety in all
things if they are looked at with extracted eyes."

CHAPTER VII

THE TRAINERS OF LICKING

I profess I was coming to feel a quiet reverence for the
common sense and quaint goodness of this people whom
I had formerly looked on as a mere agglomeration of
iniquitous savages, and for some minutes I was silent, gazing dreamily at the horrible mutilations of the battle going
on a few yards off, with the dawning conviction that there
was more in mankind than I had previously discerned.

"By the way," I finally ventured, "do you individually
teach this licking science to the whole nation?"

I saw at once that this was a very foolish question, for
had he not admitted that he knew nothing whatever about
the rules and made up a new one when his authority was
solicited? But he took my blunder leniently.

"By no means," he beamed with another rattle of his
shells. "About a fourth of the nation are set apart to
instruct the rest; the women are most serviceable in it.
All practise on the feet of the teachers, understanding that
this is only preparation; as they become more advanced
they are allowed to lap on the feet of the grandees, a special

and select preliminary to performing the act upon mine; but the highest post which a trainer can affect is overseeing the liquid maneuver on my feet and grooming the members of one who grooms mine,—he can never himself directly lick mine. Neither are the women admitted to this ineffable shekinah. The trainer is more sincere and reverential in his teaching from being barred out of its sweetest rewards; he garners his glory vicariously and can aspire only to the minor pinnacle of having it said of him in future ages that he was the teacher of a great licker. This contents him very well, for we choose the trainers from those deprecating meek obsequities who feel as much honored by a kick from a great man as they would by a country estate from a common clod-hopper. It is most interesting to see how their dutiful humility toward us grows on them with years. I have succeeded in detaching my shadow which I send through the streets on four crosspoles for the edification of the teachers, who fly forward from everywhere, prostrate themselves on the earth and lick the feet of the slaves who carry it. I sometimes secrete myself in the vicinity to observe them, for it gives me great complacence to be ocularly assured of their loyalty. A State can never fall where the educators have humble and steadfast faith in the right thing. They have succeeded in proving to the people in some manner I have not troubled to inquire into, because the first three lengths* of it wore me nearly to death, that all food, life, sunlight, and strength come out of that shadow, and are formed inside of it, according to an ingenious axiom which they have established, that everything is where it is not. Altho I don't agree with them or understand it, I believe they are right and compel my subjects to learn their ninety-six lengths on the subject by heart, and if any be so ignorant

---

*A length was a five hours' harangue without taking a fresh breath. Not all the trainers could perform a length.

as not to comprehend the reasoning, or at least not to believe in it, I degrade them into slaves."

"The trainers seem to be the very pillars of your noble savagery," said I, "and I should think you would be tender of them."

"Sir, I treat them with great gentleness and honor. They have the same privileges of punishment and death as the holder of the royal office of the feet; through my affectionate demonstrations upon their persons they may become Chancellors; and they are permitted to lick the feet of the great, which is their dream of happiness. These liberties are enough: it is a universal quality of the human bat to revere what is withheld. I should mention that the teachers are profoundly graded and are restricted to various parts of the foot to prevent their brains from growing too monotonously rich and even; the children are advanced through all the grades till they know as much as their numerous trainers combined, except the highest; they are then thirty-three years old, for they begin to study at three, but this is only the brightest, and some are seventy. Out of these bright children the advanced trainer for the great is chosen, after having approved his tenacious strength of principles by standing on one leg for seven days."

"I still fail to comprehend their state of mind, Sire," I pursued, "for on my way here from the Divinity I passed through a country where the teachers are surpassingly enlightened and gloriously independent leaders, and licking the feet of the great would be considered inadequate emolument for their conspicuous services and sacrifices, for they too save us from change and are regarded with much secret contempt by the mighty whom they sustain. This sentiment however is most scrupulously tempered in public, altho universally known to exist, for there is an unverified tradition with us that if the teachers should ever acquire a little intelligence and come into opposition to the rulers and owners of general finiteness everything old and rotten would vanish in a sudden conflagration. Therefore we feed them with cerebral pap and permit them to wear very honorable and ugly clothes so that they never mutiny. We came to this knowledge of teachers by some deep researches into monkeys and babies. These charming animals are very imitative and impressionable to exterior shows, and by similar experiments on professors we arrived at the confounding discovery that they belong to the same group. By making them think they are somebody they will repeat what we want them to say with great contentment like parrots and will chatter off our doctrines like monkeys. To make them think they are of consequence we only have to dress them in a certain ridiculous fashion. We place some cylinders of black cloth resembling flexible stove-pipes around their legs, and upon their backs and breasts a preposterous white article very stiff and uncomfortable in front, but we apply the greatest torture to their necks. These we confine in a rigid band, almost of the texture of steel, of which they can never relieve themselves in public without absolute loss of caste. The effect of this band, and of the polished flexible stove-pipes on their legs, is miraculous. The circulation of the blood through the neck is impeded so that the head, which can hardly move in its rigid casing, gets but little blood, and thus the thoughts are weak and watery just as we desire them to be. These puny thoughts can naturally grasp nothing large, and they dwell for the most part on the form and nature of the stove-pipes on their legs, their substance, creases, wrinkles, and other intricate problems of their essence. Such is their absorption in these profound monkey metaphysics that they often remain quite oblivious to hunger while we starve them to death, thinking of nothing but what they have on their necks and legs."

At these words of mine the King looked somewhat hurt.

"We are not stingy in our payments," said he; "did I not say that the children lick their trainers' feet for practice? This has a wonderfully softening spiritual effect upon the trainers, besides being held to be so flattering a boon that they accept it in lieu of half their pay. Its utility for State purposes must be as great as your civilized mind-pap and magic clothes, for while the children are thus practising the rite on their trainers' feet the latter are permitted to imagine that they are the great, which brings the trainers and the great into the most incredible sympathy and understanding. After this miraculous blending of soul with their masters our trainers never head a revolt."

While thus exchanging ideas with the King and closely attending the carnage of the aristocracy, some peculiar actions on the part of the people struck me, whose import was bewildering. The natives even down to the women and infants in arms broke up into cliques, each championing some particular great man in the heap, alive or dead, and shouting his name in unison, mingled with marrow-piercing whoops and an infernal siren whistle which seemed to start with a mild hiss far up in the air, then wailingly descending, to sweep about in riotous spirals, curves and vortices of sound, passing through the hearer like a wild scream of the tortured damned, and finally to reascend into itself on high, quavering and groaning its life out like a spent sky-rocket, a wasted volcano, or the quenched cry of a perishing steamer at sea. Each group was bursting its vitals to outscream the others and inspire its select knight, believing that a great volume of noise in the form of his name imparted physical strength. As they danced around the mass of red maggots their sympathy was metamorphosed into hate of one another, and I saw that these rival bands would soon take up the cause of their superiors on each others' heads and bring the whole tribe into the redolent plight of the forty. It was not the King's plan to have this happen

that day. With the menacing aspect of an Egyptian god
as these deities are seen in the museums, and one of the
boards of my box-cover for a weapon, he charged them with
the fury of an avalanche, surging majestically from side
to side in his royal wrath, a glorious specimen of super-
human grandeur, and soon had them chilled below fighting
heat. They nevertheless continued their wicked bellow-
ings, shaking their fists in each others' eyes and actually
cutting pieces of flesh out of their own bodies in their
uncontrollable rage, and doing themselves other execrable
injuries in their chivalrous loyalty to the august guardians
of the food and other monopolized privileges.

"What is the meaning of this, King?" I demanded when
the pandemonium lulled for breath.

"It is out tribal equality," shouted Milto back in my ear.
"The lowly identify themselves in sentiment and cheers with
some great man and in that way become a metaphorical part
of him, his equal. It is the leveling bond of sympathy, and
it levels the common and vulgar up. See how they all at
once become great by attaching themselves in spirit to the
cause of some glorious renowned individual! It is due to
the magic of love. They love and revere the virtues of
the illustrious notable whom they have adopted as the
patron of their imaginations; they live in his atmosphere,
his blood circulates theoretically through them, the oneness
is absolute, for them there is no lower or higher (which
is reserved for the high), no invidious gaps, heartburns,
or degradations, only a blur of joyous vacancy in their
mental parts. It is an ideal state and it is caused by
equality."

"Unspeakably charming!" I cried. "Poor naked savages
that you are, without capital or universities, Moses, gospel,
Greek, God, Trusts, Trousers, or lawyers, you have solved
the problem of the modern world. I suppose these great
men share everything they have with their devoted sup-

porters and live with them on terms of the sweetest intimacy."

"Bless you, no, that would be most degrading and unjust to the common people. So far as the great are concerned I can assure you they would like nothing better, but it would upset the equilibrium of the small; their heads would be turned by familiarity; they have to be kept on very short food-rations as a means of spiritual cultivation, so that it would not do to share anything with them; and the tenderest, loveliest, most delicate and precious traits of human character result from this humble state of affectionate mental dependence of the mean upon the magnificent. These people would all die for their favorite great man and would despise him as a poor-spirited impostor if he treated them kindly. It is the most beautiful exhibition of love in Africa. From time to time I let the fractious have it out among themselves: it cools their passions and quells the turbulent spirits, who generally kill each other. The contests occur in the fall when we are getting in our winter supplies of meat. We jerk the bodies and if the festivities have been spirited we are saved from going to war."

I pondered. Another lull came, and making my hands into a trumpet I yelled, "Do these great men ever do anything for the rest?"

He looked at me as a big boy does upon a small one when contemplating mischief. "They let them lick their feet," he said.

CHAPTER VIII.

My Two Miracles

The battle began to wane and I turned my mind wholly to examining the physical condition of the combatants.

Bleeding from head to foot and minus many of the ordinary signs of humanity, a stranger could not safely have said they were the remnants of human beings but only of some unclassified form of jellied biped. Several were lying dead, others with arms and legs broken or torn from the body and vital internal mishaps were writhing upon the ground emitting despairing cries. A favorite weapon had been the teeth, for nearly all were viciously lacerated in numerous parts as if masticated by wild beasts. The splendor of their incisors, the formidable prognathous structure of their jaws, and their nude exposure above and below the hip-circlet gave fearful severity to this mode of warfare.

Those who could move, about twenty in number, now stumbled forward to the baubles, and, regardless of the King's mandate that they were to take only half, incontinently seized everything that was left, each grabbing for the whole and snatching what he could get out of his neighbors' hands, until I thought the fragile stuff would be totally demolished. In this struggle the poor human scraps most depleted of blood got nothing. At this astounding appropriation there was heard a faint low respectful murmur of remonstrance from the people, entirely mild, spiritless and supplicatory, whereupon the King rose in stately fatherliness and commanded the first citizens to adjourn bloodshed and listen to him. He ordered the fighters to restore some of their plunder, that the people might have their natural share of the gift, at which a deafening shout glorifying their noble ruler as protector of the common people, as saint, Providence, equal arbiter and God, shivered the air from the multitude, who began to dance, caper and perform wonderfully, some of the specially agile climbing on to each others' shoulders four or five high, twining themselves stiffly together, and in this position turning complete somersaults, as if a lofty ladder were to do so—a feat I had not seen elsewhere and which was very fascinating.

I had much sympathy for the people whom the great
had concocted to rob so shamelessly and was glad justice
was to be done them, so I looked to see what share they
were to receive. In the mêlée some of the necklaces had
been broken, scattering the beads about, and these the great
men were now busily picking up and throwing into a tray
from the box, together with a number of pebbles of the
same size. These, as it soon appeared, were for the people.
The unimpaired necklaces, brass rings, bracelets, anklets,
eardrops, nose-rings, tin rattles, whistles, and everything
else of value, they retained for themselves. When they
had gathered up all the beads they could find, including
many that were trampled and broken, all told less than a
fiftieth of the total contents of the box, the gawded monarch benignly called his ordinary children about him, and
with royal impressiveness as if he were endowing each
with a kingdom, presented their portions of the largess
from heaven to all, amounting to two beads apiece inclusive
of the broken ones and the little stones. The populace,
nevertheless, were transcendently and pathetically delighted,
especially when informed from the impromptu throne of
my box endwise, on which His Highness squatted, tho it
wobbled much, that the heavenly sender had not stipulated
that a single bead or even a stone should go to the rabble,
but had deferred entirely to his royal wisdom and generosity to do as he pleased. By this time, having forgotten
all previous sentiments of Providence, they lifted up another
shout of glory to the King and turned more of their human-
ladder gyrations. With diaphanous complaisance the satisfied King permitted his shadow to be brought in and all
the commonalty to kiss the sole of its foot once.

In a voice that boomed over the assemblage Milto called
for the customary thanks to the divinity, which immediately
issued 'with terrific energy from the gratefully swelling
bosoms of the two-beaded multitude. He then selected

from his throat a magnificent necklace of greenish blue for his offering to deity and deposited it on a tray to encourage other givers, whereupon, for the god's use, each of the great ones drew from his stock whatever he prized least, a tin rooster, a glass marble with a spider inside, a bottle-stopper, et cetera, and joined it to the King's oblation. In their turn the common people each and all gave one of their two beads, massing them in a separate heap. Then the King, the Chief Idol-tamer, and the surviving grandees consecrated the two piles by a rite original to that land, performed by each one going through the ranks of the low-born with a receptacle of dust which stood by for the purpose and placing a handful in every native's eyes. Singular to say they all threw back their heads to receive into their open orbs and retain there the full delivery, tho the pain must have been racking. After this ceremony and the mumbling of some cabalistic noises, King Milto composedly transferred the consecrated costlier pile of his own and the great men's making to his private heap, while the great followed suit by fastening their clutches upon the rabble's consignment to the god and portioning it out among themselves. The blue-bloods fell into a minor contention over the box, which they all grossly coveted, but I firmly informed the mighty quarrel-queller that there would be no more cargoes from aloft if that vehicle were confiscated, which quickly educed from him some sparkling paradoxes, that struck a dozen of the grasping patricians wittily between the eyes and sent them rolling a distance.

Mounting again on Majesty's back, which seemed to have a cataleptic effect on the mob, I declared from this rostrum that the day's adventures would close with a couple of original miracles. Tipping the box on its end that all might see the empty interior I called them to witness that there was nothing within. Directing the King and his deputies to apply the dust to the public optics as before, this time not omitting their own eyes, I removed a false bottom, beneath which was stowed a quantity of candy drops, very hard, powerfully flavored, and colored and shaped like beads; then ordering the people to wipe out the dust I displayed my creation to their tearfully astonished sight. The great men were about to rush in for a sweeping consolidation of it, according to law and order and custom, but I waved them off with authority born of the miracle, which had wrought a deep impression.

"Now for the second miracle," said I. "These beads shall be changed into a very delightful food which you can all eat." I lifted my right leg into the air three times and when it was at right angles to my body waved the foot on its axis six times and touched the sole with my little finger; I then directed King Milto, who, on account of his elevated intelligence through which he could see farther into the occult than most, was more amazed by these marvels than the rest, to distribute the enchanted articles to the people.

"And," I said emphatically, "by god's will, with no meddling of earthly charity associated or otherwise, every man, woman and child from Your Highness down to that six-legged dwarf is to have the same number of them."

I had a mysterious purpose in this which will appear in the sequel. It was the first time they had tasted American sweets and their faces shone with a happiness I never expect to see again in this world.

Having sent the box to the King's private cave for safe storage, attention was paid to the twenty great characters who since the terrible battle had been left unnoticed where they fell. Four were dead; the others, among them the 'King's Feet' and the Cook of Natives, were so shattered inside and out that the King ordered them to be dispatched and a public repast of the bodies proclaimed in honor of all gods who possess things that men want to get. At the end of the feast the finger- and toe-nails of the departed were presented as a special contribution to the non-gift-giving gods.

CHAPTER IX

The King and I Sit in a Tree

My position was now established as only second to that of the monarch himself, and on the following day Milto announced with a thousand marks of affection and confidence that the office of the Feet was vacant for me if I would be so good as to accept it, signifying also that I should be promoted as speedily as possible to the Council of the Ancients. The proposition filled me with untold anxieties as to what they might now expect of me, having seen my miraculous powers verified. It was plain enough that the King had warmly set his heart on having me lick his basic elements; yet I doubted if this was entirely disinterested, for he could not but perceive how vastly my prestige was expanding.

"Your Lambent Sagacity overlooks the danger to the peace and regularity of the realm in this new precedent," I expostulated; "I have had no training for such a load of duty, and if you advanced me to that dizzy honor without a thirty years' course, every Tom, Jim and Jake you have would think the same preference belonged to him and your institutions would soon be nourishing the worms. Let me graduate first, for precedent is paramount in licking as it is in other matters of State and tribunals of Justice."

This presentment put him off for the time being, but I saw trouble ahead. I therefore resolved to forestall him.

The next day we were seated together in the branches of a tree commanding his domain, chatting amiably over a plan of his to capture a white caravan that was beating its course toward the interior.

"By the way," said I, "this morning I had a letter from the Origin of that box of gifts."

"Um, you did? Anything new in the universe?"

"He sent sharp orders. He's getting the next exhibit ready, but He says you must go to work on your part of the contract."

"Go ahead," said the monarch with forced composure, "what are we to do?"

"You are to make me Improver of the Earth."

"I can soon do that," he exploded, relieved, "it will help us; what else?"

"Wait till you know the qualities of Improver of the Earth before you exult," I admonished, "and appoint me now."

"Well?"

"It's a higher position than officer of your feet," I said, to deal a hard blow.

He winced visibly, then asked, "Who is this meddlesome god that demands so much of me?"

"The one that gives you so much. Among the celestials he goes by the name 'Eternal Order of Things.'"

"I like the sound of that," Milto ruminated; "it doesn't seem that one with so good a name could do anything improper."

"Even to speak of such a possibility of 'Eternal Order' is to blaspheme," I frowned, and he cowered.

"I appoint you Improver of the Earth; impart what the god wants of me next."

"I'm going to perform another miracle, and show you how to obtain beautiful yellow grains called 'gold' out of common dirt. Then your whole tribe, under your leading, may amuse yourselves executing this miracle every day for the sake of your god and me."

"Am I to have some of this divine substance?"

"You truly call it divine. Without it there could be no

heaven that men would desire; gods would be vulgar objects if they could not show their superiority by parading themselves in gold and diamonds, and as soon as men acquire sufficient gold they become possessed of every essential attribute of gods. If you are gentle, loving and obedient to my will, I may hereafter grant you a portion of this elixir of divinity, as a condescension tho not as a right, but you must carefully refrain from all avarice to own it, since that is forbidden by religion. Religion is so made that we must not crave the thing for which the illustrious gods are chiefly celebrated, for they cannot part with their essence without loss, and men must console themselves with copying the divinities in the minor things—their virtues. You are aware also that you have made me developer of your earth, and if I permit you to live in your country after that it is uncommonly generous on my part, without my giving you a share of the gold it contains. You are to dig that in return for the privilege of staying where you are, as you will fully understand when you have thoroughly studied the character of your Bountiful Providence, the Eternal Order of Things, the One Buzzrack, to whom I have just introduced you. It is my design to exhibit elements of his nature to you in sermons when you are too weary to work, for I am accurately instructed in it, and if you ever feel inclined to complain of your lot you will learn from my preaching that it is a sin to resist the heavenly will as it is revealed by those who love you and understand heaven best. Being robbed by your betters on earth is the straight and narrow path to paradise, where I haven't any doubt you will be allowed to scrub the floors for the better angels."

This was so reasonable that the King readily consented and promised to interpret my generosity to his countrymen, which I exhorted him to do very explicitly in the simplest Rinyoese that there might not arise a misunderstanding as to the ownership of things.

We crawled down from the tree, in which I was feeling rather stiff, and I suggested a promenade through the realm. Some of the customs of the tribe had seemed very novel to me, but my mind up to this time having been much occupied with my own safety I had not delved into them. Feeling now more secure I could look about with a careless and interested eye as we ambled along.

"Why do so many of your people wear those long and heavy poles of different lengths fastened horizontally across the small of their backs? Not a few of them, I notice, can scarcely walk under the load."

"That is our visible emblem of learning, lineage, and dignity. The longer and heavier it is, the greater you may know is the bearer of it: that is to say, the farther advanced in the knowledge of the great Science of My Feet, Respectability."

"It must be very inconvenient, people cannot come anywhere near each other with those remarkable appurtenances on."

"That is the design. It prevents the low and ignorant from contact with the learned and high, for of course they have to walk around each other by the distance of the poles they wear."

"Doesn't it keep equals apart also? I should think they would be lonesome without closer companionship than these poles suffer."

"That is a necessary precaution for preserving life. The equally great and learned are bitterly jealous of one another, if permitted to come together they froth, and if not separated they bite and murder."

He explained further that in wars the poles were only worn by the officers, who could not be defiled by coming into contact with the enemy as they might be obliged to do if the poles were discarded.

CHAPTER X

THE LONG POLES. I AM CONDEMNED TO DEATH

The gold digging began very auspiciously, except for the fact that the poles were much in the way and impeded work. Not less than nine-tenths of the productive energy of the tribe was lost, since not only did the weight of them hinder motion, frequently causing their wearers to fall forward in a helpless heap, whence they could only be got upright again by the aid of those who had not yet fallen down, when it would be a wonder if the would-be rescuers did not measure themselves out on top of the others, consuming nearly all the time not in getting gold but in falling down and getting up, but in addition to this there could be but little helpful assistance in labor rendered by one to another, since unless one were stretched out useless on the earth none could approach him to co-operate or even to pass by with a load. With things in this plight, although the whole population including the King, his wives and concubines and the principal men endeavored to work from the moment the sun assumed the scepter of day until he laid it down at night for repose, mighty little gold was realized. Upon my pointing this out to His Majesty and suggesting that the poles be laid aside during working hours, he assured me that there would certainly be a terrible revolution if the attempt were made, in the course of which he would be deposed and devoured with me in a side dish, and that they would then be sure to select a King who would double the length of the poles for the sake of popularity.

So we labored along for a week with a flickering zest on the part of the tribe, I myself sitting on a shaded eminence and directing maneuvers, yet with no practical results to speak of. The ground was teeming with gold, but at this rate it would take four generations to get out the quantity needed to make a small millionaire.

"Your licking custom is a great crime," I declared to the King with choler when Saturday night came and we had all laid aside our tools until Monday morning in order to attend the church which I had established. "Between licking and the long poles it is the silliest foolery practised by honest men in the circle of our solar system; but I would care nothing for that: so long as it didn't interfere with the progress of civilization you might lick and be hanged, or carry pine trees on your backs and sprint, never would I oppose the genius of your institutions; but when you block the advancement of liberal ideas with your poles, and hinder the spread of perfection over the globe by your licking, it is time for righteousness to be bold. However necessary these instrumentalities may be for the culture of the privileged or restraint of the natural selfishness and inborn brutality of your masses, for the sake of the world they must be cast aside. I came here unselfishly to collect gold for the purpose of promoting the Kingdom of Good in the United States by greasing the wheels of greed. But look at this little basketful of the yellow god-stuff: it doesn't amount to a thousand dollars, which wouldn't gild a god's little finger tip, and that's the only result of a hard week's toil. If you are afraid to abolish pole-wearing alone, how would it do to brush away the whole licking ceremony and fly into the van of human development at one bound?"

I think if His Majesty had not been physically lame and mentally limp from his unusual week's usefulness there would have been trouble between us. He choked down his irritation and replied patiently.

"You do not know what you suggest; you would tear down the free fabric of our commonwealth; without the study and practice of licking, without these poles to publicly herald the progress of each in this noble work, without the honorable names formed from the number of rins' length these poles contain, what object would my people have in life? They would renounce all obligations and obedience, abandon themselves to ghastly infamy, embrace abominable license, devote their powers to self-destruction in nameless orgies, for that is the law of human nature when it gets loose from its serious institutions. The keenest pleasure my people have is that of comparing the length of their poles and finding some longer than others; nor without these visible emblems of exaltation to struggle for do I know of a single potent stimulus to effort. All human initiative springs from them; bereft of their magic impetus we should starve, because there would be no incentive to work. The beasts of the forest would cease to envy and emulate us."

Even in my vexation I could not forbear asking what connection rins had with names, and was richly rewarded for my curiosity when I heard the following:

A rin was their unit of measure, slightly more than our foot. They estimated human greatness as spatial, and most accurately measured by length; as a man became greater he naturally would become larger to display it, but here nature defaulted, for the great did not grow larger, and the poles were brought in to correct nature's defect. The name followed the pole in length. If a man's pole was one rin long his name was Rin; if five rins, it was Rin-Rin-Rin-Rin-Rin; if one hundred or a thousand rins, it was Rin repeated as many times. Since there was no sound in the entire vocabulary of names but rin, people were distinguished from one another not by divers sounds as with us, but by the number of these rins they were entitled to be called, and their names changed and enlarged as they grew greater. It was one of the strictest etiquets of the land that when a great or big personage was addressed

his full name was to be pronounced unless the bitterest
insolence were designed, that is to say, he could not be
spoken to as Thirty Rins, but as Rin pronounced separately
thirty times in succession. To omit one was equivalent to
stepping on his toes or spitting in his face. Thus familiarity of intercourse from the low toward the high was dis-
couraged by the labor of approach; thus conversation between the great was rendered easy and affable, as they
spent most of their time in the dignified ceremony of addressing each other by name. Flatterers who wished to
ingratiate themselves with the great followed them about
enunciating their syllables, to keep them conscious of their
extent; and they had a machine which said Rin and could
be so adjusted as to recite a man's name, pause a moment
and begin again, by the musical self-adulation of which
the great were wont to sink to sleep. While an American
would be improving himself reading in his family newspaper about the latest murders, the Rinyo would serenely
sit listening to his name in this machine. When a guest
visited an aristocrat the speaking machine was altered to
the number of his rins in welcome, and then made to alter-
nate the names of visitor and host, thus carrying on a glowing conversation back and forth for any length of time
without exertion of the great men's intellects or vocal
organs. Titles learned and aristocratical were held in de-
rision there as opposed to the democratic simplicity of the
country; all were recognized as equal and alike because the
basis of the names of all was Rin.

It was trying. Here at my feet lay the princely material
for a thousand multi-millionaires, and I was prevented
from gathering it by a brace of mammoth farces which this
benighted anthropophagus called social institutions! I
could have trampled on him, in theory. A better plan suggested itself.

"Why not," I proposed, "invent some useful practice to

take the place of these outrageous abortions, these hollow distortionate follies for which there are no suitable words in my mind, something that would represent real worth and do the people's souls good in the performance?"

He replied: "Tell me, cloud-born ambassador, if you know human weaknesses as well as one in your high office should, what custom could be more perfectly suited to a humanity composed of mud and murder than one which fully accomplishes its end and leaves no restive surplus energy or thought behind to trouble rulers? These marvelous habits of the tongue and pole are fitted to the soul of man like skin to his flesh; all the pulsing yearnings and vasty attributes of his nature are satisfied; in what he does it is true there is no invasion of intelligence, but no intelligence is there to invade; becheated to be sure through all his bootless days, I acknowledge that he is forever kept in the midnight zone of the quadrupedal brutes, but is not his life filled and cloyed with his deeds of crazy foolishness? And can you say more of any people? Are not his brain and body busied to repletion? He makes no trouble, and does not our political system flourish unimpaired forever? If I can raise a towering, noble, proud, imposing hierarchy on the grotesque glittering humbug of licking my stainless feet, and elevate cringing licking into the grandest principle of human conduct, dignify it as a system and saturate my kind with a reverential sense of its mystery and majesty, if I can guilefully entice all creeping human things to extinguish their strength in spurious education for this fulsome licking, and fix a terrible pole upon their backs to indicate and blazon their proficiency and drain off their strength in blisters, and let them add seventy rins or more together to construct their names, and they do not perceive that they belong to the glorified kingdom of imbeciles, asses and bats, than whom the born dead are more rational because they do nothing, what more can you ask of a cus-

tom? Have customs any other use? Were you ever in
a better regulated society? And is not that the summum
bonum of savagery? Do not our people work from the
first crowing of the eastern sun till it recalls its flock
of beams into the silent hennery of night, for the customary
stipend of emptiness, sickness, sorrow, poverty and death?
Do they not fulfil man's proper destiny? Do they know
what it is to think, hold up their heads without an irresistible desire to fawn upon and lick a fellow cannibal, or
stretch their limbs and run at liberty without those deadly
poles to cover them with sores and break their backs? No.
If they knew that they are fools, I do not see what would
become of society; government could not be carried on a
day; humanity would fly apart into murderously discordant
atoms. And, truth is, they are all now as happy as can be:
while doing reasonable and sensible things would crush
them down in suicidal desolation." A look of real affection
came into the great Crowned Head's eyes as he spoke these
grand truths, and I loved him.

I spent Sunday considering how to meet the business
crisis, even refraining from going up in the afternoon to
hear the guardian of the idol Iztaph give a public disquisi-
tion on the beauty of that deity's face, which looked to me
like the battered front of a stove. He was the god of art,
I believe. They kindled a fire in the idol's mouth whenever
he was to be esthetically shown off. The pole of the guardian of this wonderful object was so long that no one
could come within the sound of his voice, nevertheless all
the tribe were required to attend the exhibition or lose
their heads. Having cleared not so much as a thousand
dollars the previous week I was angry enough to take the
risk of decapitation. At about four o'clock—they always
had a late dinner on Sunday owing to the elongated eloquence of the Idol-Guard—King Milto came toward my
apartment with several athletes bearing the decapitation

apparatus. He was in a famished mood and his native instincts were choking down the Christian impulses I had stowed away in him; he was counting on me for the Sunday roast. I took a desperate resolution as they approached on the run. Drawing a dozen sulphurous and deadly cigars from a pocket in the rock where I had them secreted, and an innocent and delicious one from my case, I lighted the latter and began to puff volcanically.

"Hold!" cried I as they thundered up, "I am communing with our deity: whoever enters my office without this talisman in his mouth will be struck dead."

They were a superstitious crew to whom tobacco smoking was still to be revealed, and they recoiled in dread at my threat.

"I know your purpose," continued I, "and we shall see if it meets with the favor of Omnipotent Nothing. Sample this weed, and if it agrees with your stomachs the Eternally Hidden is pleased, if not he is offended at your conspiracy against my life, and you will have to take your chopping machine home."

Lighting the cigars, which were saturated with powerful ingredients, for one must never go as a missionary without a few contrivances to wheedle destiny, I handed them around and awaited results. They were not slow in coming. While the awful monarch and his nobility lay on my floor weltering in their indiscretion, I smoked on with my usual pleasure in the sustaining fruit, verifying my claim to a cloudy extraction. The African system in those parts is sadly affected by drugs if they be choice and powerful—almost as by deadly poisons. Seeing them so livid and retched I dragged them out into the fresh peace of the Sabbath afternoon and hurriedly sent for the national rubbers to seduce their coagulating blood into circulation. Terrified crowds came hurrying in great panic on learning that their beloved King had fallen in a fit, nor had any the strength to rub, in their dread of his impending dissolution. They thought if he departed there would be a final winding up of things, that the light would vanish and the sun cease to blush in heaven, and that their food supply would depart in company with his defunct essence. These seem to be the religious tenets of warm countries, eradicable I suspect only by killing a new king each day for many years as a lesson. Taking advantage of their stupefaction I explained that their royal earthly father was being chastened by their heavenly one for offensive designs on my life, and assured them that the same condign discipline would overtake them all if the attempted profanation of me recurred. I then gave His Majesty morphine and soon had him comfortably snoring.

CHAPTER XI

I Begin to Civilize the Rinyos

Milto was able to sit up the next day but not to work, so we made a holiday of it, I improving the idleness to expatiate upon the decision I had formed.

"These poles," said I, "must come off during working hours, I am resolved upon that. In working hours there is equality of all before the employer. The Law of Work, and the fact that you all work for me settle that. It is an undisputed fact in the first theologies that if a number of unequal persons love the same Being they are thereby made equal among themselves by an invisible theological equality. It doesn't affect life. So it is in Toil. If they work for the same being they likewise become equal to each other while they work. The law of work clearly enunciates that whoever works for a master shall expend all his strength—now the exertion put forth by all is thus equal, though they may not possess equal force, and by this doctrine of equal exertion all workers are brought to a level. To enforce my decision and convince the people that my authority is supreme, on the morrow you must lick my feet in the presence of the host, for since I am Proprietor of the Earth, I am lord of all that is upon it, yourself and your tribe with the rest."

Milto could not seem to digest this caustic proposition; I dreaded his balking at this stage. It is one of a missionary's chief tribulations that a savage is wanting in mental background. I am convinced that there are no inborn ideas of natural right, at least not in savages. (Those of natural wrong are numerous.) If there were, Milto would have seen that having ceded the development of the earth to me he thenceforth dwelt upon it and breathed its air by my merciful forbearance. I bore him no illwill, but I firmly desired what was mine. Before I came into possession of the earth his right to live on it was as good and free as anyone's; now however that the control of the earth was mine, he must earn his right to live; he no longer possessed anything inalienable but the right to earn, and not that unless I supplied him with it. He was in no sense my slave, he might wander forth into the desert with his tribe to found some new realm, for my conscience was clear on the point that he had not conveyed to me the whole of Africa, nor his body. I was morally proud to inform him that he was free. His body was still his own—not in continuity, which would have implied a right to something to continue it on, but simply so long as it could persist with the food and vital fire stored already inside it. To this plain distinction, resting deep in the fiber of human prosperity, I invited Milto's prayerful reflection. I was sorry he had no lawyers to reflect and pray with him. I showed him that the sacred rights of human freedom, won chiefly at Bunker Hill I believe, would allow him to wander through the world along the sweet paths of his infancy, unmolested, unshot, unimprisoned for theft, if he kept his hands off the food that he had transferred to me as earth's proprietor. "What more can you wish?" said I,—"nothing is more perfect than perfect freedom. You have a free body, make the most of it while it lasts, which will be from twenty to forty days if you avoid exercise. There is a difference as large as the decalogue between the freedom to saunter across the world in any direction that you love, while the food within you holds out, and the right to feed yourself anew from food not in you, when you have made over the earth to a more thrifty and deserving neighbor."

Still, if he had emigrated he would have done me a ghastly injustice and I should have had a grudge against him; his cession of the care of the earth was of limited value if he did not stay to work upon it for me, which I considered that he had tacitly pledged to do when he established me as its master. A section of this lowly foot-stool is of little worth if those on it are not of normal formation; they must be powerfully attached to their birth-place, that they may be willing to work for the new owner without stipulating for profit if he magnanimously grants them the occupancy of the spot where their free ancestors lived and laughed and reveled and died. I conceive that when descendants refuse to do this they very ungratefully if not criminally attack property rights. I had accepted the position of master of the Rinyo soil in good faith, in return for it intending to give them the blessings of new ideas, far away from home, at the sacrifice of my comfort and pleasure, postponing marriage and a seat in the senate; I was instructing them in the new duties which the higher moral sphere upon which they had embarked entailed; I was teaching them to know mine from thine, particularly mine and not thine, if not for their use and advantage in this world, at least that they might enter the society of civilized persons in the life to come without ignorance and embarrassment. I demanded common requital, all that they had was enough, and that was legally mine; I resolved to plant the incurable seeds of civilization in their substance and leave Providence to do the watering, to make them sprout into a race like the Americans, if He cared for another of that brand.

The distinguished monarch broke the silence with an uncertain voice: "I made you Developer of the Earth, did I not? And if I created you to that position am I not higher than you?"

"You were, but are so no longer, since you made me higher; Developer of the Earth is the highest place there can be; if you decline to consider me paramount, having made me so, it refutes your paramountcy, it cuts a gash in your absolute authority, all your acts and decrees will be despised as impotent if this one is so. You elevated me into the mastership of the earth and all the measureless rights of that dignity; you must hereafter bow to, worship and obey me, enforcing equal veneration on your subjects, for it is clearly to be seen that is your authority unequal to the exact extortion of your personal behests it is good for nothing. Having lifted me to the loftiest promontory of power you preserve lordship over me by obeying me, because you are then paying obedience to yourself; but, having raised me up, if you fail in obedience you launch a thrust at your perfect prestige; for when, having placed another's foot on your neck, you falter and fail to keep it there, lo it is your own priceless predominance that you impugn. So in order to maintain your supremacy you must hold me principal and supreme over you, in all acts doing faithful service and obedience to myself as your chief; and in my despotic autocracy I shall be only supporting, illustrating and confirming your sovereignty, which made me what I am. I shall see that you serve me faithfully and docilely, in doing so adding brighter luster to your superlative self."

He was convicted by this unanswerable blending of poetry and logic, as of course I knew he would be, since it has conquered shrewd civilized men thousands of times in the name of the State, and on the morrow he walked feebly to the works and declared himself my leal subject by licking my feet before the devoted eyes of the concourse. In the melodic Rinyoese I had framed for him he recited the royal manifesto covenanting that as master of the earth I became principal in power through the efficacy of his mighty high inviolable edict, that unless I was super-lord over the earth and everything in and on it including him, his subjects and his expectations, he, my maker, would cease to be sovereign; and at my extempore instigation he also expounded how he, as embodiment, essence, soul and life of the people, according to proper theories of government, acted for them all in this circumstance and carried their submission in his deed. To make assurance secure I suggested that the council of the superannuate sages be called in to ratify the proceeding, which was done with the aid of wheelbarrows. The tribe took the whole in good part, encouraging me by their good humor to broach my clever design against the poles. It was no less impolitic than inhuman to fly in the face of their deeper instincts when a wise head could make them pull together in the interest of civilization; it was not best to eradicate their impulse to lick, but to turn it into one of the world's broad channels and extract the private fortunes happily saturating it. The licking habit should be made to dredge my gold.

I had triumphed over the King through the power of conscience. I wrote a paragraph in my journal to show that savages respond to intelligent arguments, they yield to motives of duty if its finer shades are patiently disclosed, by sheer force of character I had subjugated the brute

propensities of this fierce King; high principle always sub-
dues low principle or unprinciple, thought I; I remembered
that a successful American moralist of pleasing ability and
a power to see more sides of everything than it possessed,
had described character as of a stellar and undiminishable
greatness; he said of the man of character that 'his vic-
tories are by demonstration of superiority, and not by
crossing of bayonets—he conquers because his arrival alters
the face of affairs,' and this beautiful thought, I said, shall
be my light and guidance here.   Thus inspired I addressed
the throng.

"In labor," said I in tones of euphonious persuasion, "all
men are equal; it is only in the attributes of idleness and
uselessness that they are unequal and superior one over.an-
other; those who are idlest are always the greatest, and in
all times and places the most useless are those most highly
praised and reverenced and pampered by their fellows.
This is part of the perfect plan installed by the Promoter
of Creation, for had it not been so would this beautiful
custom always have prevailed over the earth?   It is by this
argument that we prove God's existence, for when we consider the terrible condition of mankind we understand that
the greatest being in the universe is also the idlest.   And
the same principle establishes the sanctity of all the world's
rottenness.   Being equal while you work, and all standing
upon the lowest level known to man or ape, you can lay
aside your poles, to compensate for which I will permit you
to wear them in your sleep, a time of conspicuous idleness
and greatness, and vouchsafe to you several other privileges, while on your part you must steadfastly pursue your
education in licking to prepare yourselves to work for me
more ably and intelligently.   Those who make the greatest
progress in licking shall do ever less of the work, until the
perfect in that discipline, the King's Feet and the Forty
Respectables, shall be altogether exempt from useful toil

and do nothing but wear their poles and walk in the presence of the laborious multitude to create envy and stimulate exertion."

I was here interrupted by a frenzied huzza, from which it was evident that they fell in with the pregnant modern idea that while successful licking is the best schooling for all work, its proper reward is the privilege of doing nothing and of rendering the toil of others as bitter as possible. Having baited this several-pronged hook with more freshly killed syllogisms I conceived that they would be as tame as I could desire.

To complete the new social system I was founding on the bulwarks of civilization, I increased the dimensions of their poles four times, which caused them to nearly expire with weight and happiness, and to experience the same satisfaction from wearing them a little while that they had formerly derived from doing so the entire day. This end was further promoted by an ordinance I published permitting them all to appear in a public place after supper and the end of the day's work with their poles on their haunches. Upon this terrace they strutted up and down at pole distance from one another, dolefully dragged out in aspect, yet swaggering mightily, never exchanging a word, many of them so weary with the day's gold-seeking and the gravity of the poles that they could hardly stand up, enjoying the isolation and relative superiority over those below them extremely. Even the shortest-poled ones, the most spurned and meanest of all, having no superiority over any one to brag about, manifested a truculent pride in the superiority of their inferiority.

They eagerly adopted the proposition of wearing their poles to bed, although it was accompanied with some inconveniences. They could only sleep in one position, namely upon their backs, for if they tried it on their stomachs the poles' weight soon drove them again to their backs.

Even in the latter position it was quite painful to have so considerable a hump in the small of their spinal column to lie upon, as any of you may discover for himself by trying it with a stick of wood. Naturally their rest was badly broken, as I could see by their sunken eyes, haggard looks, the distress to their health, but their happiness was touchingly increased and I thought their working powers would last, till as much gold was mined as I could handle.

My decree upon second thought, that the best educated, the Illustrious in fact, including the King, were not to work at all, but should spend the days promenading forward and backward on an eminence in the presence of the diggers, that the latter might envy them and work with more spirit, proved a most brilliant conception. They were to walk on certain lines marked out for them, from which they could not deviate without degradation; their poles being the largest of all were of such fearful pressure that merely to lift them was a dangerous strain, but the grand characters never faltered the whole day through, carrying them up and down, streaming with perspiration and deadly faint with fatigue, sustained by the consciousness of their exaltation and nerved by the excruciating duties of their fastidious sphere. From time to time one died, only to leave his place to be begged for by a hundred passionate applicants. In fact, by my astute arrangement of the poles, the grandees worked harder than the wretches who were clawing out the gold, but since their efforts were connected solely with honor, and producd no product but envy, they were humbled and adulterated with none of the repugnant attributes of labor. Once each day I had the King publicly lick my feet to testify that our compact of my supremacy was inviolable. He had never worked or borne a pole before and it wore on him; I figured that it would not be many years before he could creditably join the council of the centuries.

With the gold, however, we made splendid speed under
the new régime, the second week bringing in a mighty pile
of riches. When you reflect that I paid the people nothing,
merely permitting them to collect their scraps of food at
odd times or to wheedle a small supply out of the women—
if they could ever be enticed away from a peculiar inexpli-
cable feminine occupation of theirs connected with leaves—
and to sleep on the earth, you may agree with me that I was
a good business man. An acre lot is a fine bed, sometimes
moist and springy, and this furniture was cheap and plenty.
The gradations of honor which I had affixed to them, and
the various ranks of jealousy portioned out with nice perception, were ample tether to hold the race tramping round
the treadmill goal of duty. Lest the tropical abundance of
their passions and their unregenerate love of liberty should
impel them to error, I kept them well jaded with honest
toil and their evening recreation with the poles, so that
they hadn't a spark of fire for revolution or righteousness
even if they had known what these were.

CHAPTER XII

The White Caravan

The day was approaching when the caravan of white
prospectors was to pass near the King's realm on its way
to the deeper interior for gold. The King's scouts continually informed him of its progress and reported the minute
details of its composition. There were twenty white men
in the company, with twice as many native servants and
guides; the whites, said our scouts, carried something resembling their poles, but no longer than the shortest, which
sometimes made a terrible noise, and smoked as I had done
at the time of the King's disease, whence the spies con-

cluded that they were all gods like myself. These commercial pilgrims, the first that had ever entered that country, for my design in coming was rather Biblical than mercenary, were bearing fifty miles to the south of our nation, ignorant of the gold which it sheltered. There was nothing to be feared from them; however it suited both the King's plans and my own, for diverse reasons, that they should be destroyed. He craved a supply of human meat of some new variety and a holiday from the drudgery I was imposing, as well as the camels and general plunder; I coveted their picks and shovels and other gold-getting implements, fearing also that they might survive to return our way and confiscate the millions I was amassing. Nevertheless, for politic reasons I would not assume responsibility for the attack, nor did I intend to be visible in the campaign. If any of the immigrants fled back to the coast and returned with an English host to exterminate the Rinyo tribe for discipline and take their gold for indemnity, I wished to be sincerely able to say that I was a prisoner there working under the greed and constraint of a cruel nigger King. At the same time I shrewdly planned the onslaught for His Royal Highness so that none of his enemies might escape.

When he came to me for permission to strike work for several days to conduct this excursion—it was his custom now to rely on me in the main in all matters—I assured him the affair of the caravan was in his hands, not mine, that I was ignorant of the customs of his people in regard to the treatment of caravans and could not interfere, that as a missionary I wished to be governed as far as possible in my conduct by their moral code, for I considered that whatever morality had naturally grown up in a region was suited to and right for that region, and that if they came to believe on the Lord Jesus Christ as I hoped in time they would from seeing my prosperity, details of moral action would not count at all on the Judgment Day, that I would accompany them to the scene of crime disguised as a savage and under his orders.

There was a small desert in the invaders' line of march, with an oasis near the center; it was here that their guides planned a camp for the night and here that by my suggestion King Milto projected a thoroughly artistic slaughter. I prompted him to throw forward a thousand of his trustiest warriors, who should secrete themselves in the trees immediately environing the spring of the oasis, whence they could let themselves drop suddenly upon the newly arrived company while they were drinking, catching them off their guard and weary, with their arms laid aside. A large body of troops was to encircle the entire green island in careful seclusion, so that if a single fugitive, white or black, escaped he might be expeditiously slain. With five thousand infantry, part of whom were women, the flower of his battalions, the King in person was to lie waiting in the vicinity of the spring and all were to cry out ferociously when their comrades leaped from the trees, to increase the consternation. I deemed that it would be an exceedingly well-balanced caravan to resist these engines of confusion, and happily this one was not made for extraordinary achievements. There were few heroes in it, for all succumbed shamefully to the first blow on the back; every man of it fell by the spear, or, if I am more literal, being already fallen down to drink, the spear transfixed him to the earth, and our army came off unscratched but for a few broken bones acquired in falling from the trees. Through this amazing exploit I approached nearer than ever in the benighted minds of my adopted countrymen to absolute identity with the Infinite Ether. I held a praise meeting which led to some spiritual results I am bound to believe; at all events it introduced a good custom and was the foundation of religious revivals in that Principality. There was glorious plunder, both in gold-digging and transportation material of the kind I should need for moving my golden masses, and in kickshaws such as the natives valued far above the things of the spirit and all those of real import in connection with human progress. As I witnessed them transported with joy over their fabulous nothings, I almost wished I might throw off the load of human responsibility resting upon me and my race as advance agents of peace, happiness, clothes, wages, school books, Christ, alcohol, tuberculosis and syphilis, to enjoy untrammeled the serene primal sensation of simple living. . 'Were it not for the noble part my gold is to play in the enlightenment of the world,' I reflected, 'giving employment and food to many poor persons otherwise doomed to starve because the good have taken their property, turning the wheels of large and useful machines, calming the fiery avarice of my relatives and thus bringing them into harmony with Eternal Love, reproving those of my friends who doubted the utility of a college education, restoring confidence in the ministry as a practical avenue for intellect and heart, leading mankind up through the enjoyment of marvelous riches to a better appreciation of Heaven and a stronger desire to so live in the practice of great functions on earth as to be worthy of greater ones in Heaven, I verily believe I should lay aside all to live in humble contentment, perhaps joining myself to this flexible race for good and all and exerting my symmetrical talents to prune away their follies and preserve and fecundate their sweet natural genius. But this I know to be a moral weakness; it is shirking the duty which one owes to the cellular hypothesis. Fundamental black protoplasm, just starting to creep toward self-discovery in the tardy types of men, irrespective of its race or acquired proclivities, is to be shoveled on to the car of civilization if it is pliant, if not, it is to be ground under the wheels of Christian love or stuffed into the red-hot furnace of infinite

mercy to propel the mighty harmonious engines of good.
I am not here doing this work altogether because I desire
to, although this desire outweighs all my other moods; I am
certainly directed by the will of Heaven; I feel it; no one
manufactures his own wishes, they are implanted in him
from above, for my blessed religion teaches that God thus
inwardly communicates with and guides his believing
children.'

You see, gentlemen, I am no pessimist and am a very
great philosopher. Man's true heavenly lord and guide is
his strongest passion; theologians of an earlier age taught
the supremacy of a still small voice called conscience, but
I see no evidence in the dealings of my beloved Maker that
the weak things or voices are intended to control the loud
and strong; that sedate little dwarf appendix is meant only
for a momentary inhibition of action until we can decide
among our strong desires which is the strongest, and rest
assured that when we follow that we are sailing on the
bosom of God's will, steered by His Grace. *My* strongest
desire is for gold; I prefer it before friends, or ease, or any
quality of soul that I have seen mentioned in the best sacred
or poetical works; what then can be more evident than God's
intention to work out the good of the world through my
pursuit of gold? Did He not implant the thirst for this
superlative substance in me? And did He do it by mistake?
Was He ignorant of his business? Not at all. I am
delegated, like others with the same heaven-given instinct, to transform the face of the earth; it is the next
stage of redemption in God's wise foresight to save the
world by infinitesimal degrees. The world will be saved
just before it ends. The passion for gold being placed in
the strongest men and in the largest number, will win, over
such feeble ardors as peace, good will, fraternity, duty,
humanity and love, showing that it is Jehovah's purpose to
steep the soul of man in greed, cruelty and crime, prepar-

atory to the eternal life of brotherly love in Heaven. Heaven may bloom on earth when the world is a trifle superannuated and mankind gibberingly senile, a few hundred centuries down the whitening slope of time. But I do not presume to fathom God, which is not a practical business proposition, and is possibly insulting to His depth; I do His will as manifested in the stoutest passions of my nature, trusting His infinite grace to perfect my heart and the souls of the men I destroy, through his holy inscrutable ways. When I chat with Him at the throne He will explain all. Even the sandbag may be an instrument of divine glory in the right hands. The broken and contrite heart and the battered and bleeding head are often paths to the same perfection. Since God teaches us everything by sorrow we ought not to hesitate to hammer happiness into the weak by making them as miserable as we can. Pardon this digression, it may be of service as the history proceeds.

CHAPTER XIII

REBELLION

Digging went on much faster than before in consequence of the tools, so fast indeed that I estimated I should in a few months have all the ripe riches I could carry from the country with the national stock of camels and mules. The wonders derived from the caravan somewhat eclipsed my next galaxy of toys, unearthed and distributed with the same ceremony as before, but it kept up the diversion, greasing the machinery of things reasonably for about two weeks, when there were new mutterings of rebellion.

"This must be nipped in the bud, King," I said sternly, "it is a wanton outburst against your merciful rule, since I am doing business under your appointment and guaran-

tee. You conferred on me the privilege of making your
subjects work, and pledged that all movements, mobs, eruptions, aspirations and disorders should be put down. I call
on you to keep your promise, to save yourself from being
publicly despised by the conspirators as weak and soft. No
government can stand an instant which coddles conspirators against itself. It is incumbent on you to resent this
indignity and quell the outbreak."

Although nearly absolute master of the King and holding him with a fascinating hypnotism of conscience in all
that concerned the people, I was sedulous to have the orders
apparently emanate from His Majesty, whom they obeyed
with organic instinct. Several incipient rebellions of the
most ominous description were stifled in this way, a number
of the frailer subjects requiring to be publicly hanged—for
I was scrupulous to introduce beneficent civilization in
healthy discipline as well as in daily delights—before they
gained an inkling of their duty to yield lawful obedience
to the mandates of the new State composed of me, yet despite this the perilous outbreaks increased until I could not
sleep from fear that the following day would suffer from
my destruction. I did not fear death, but I felt I owed it
to Heaven, who had placed so much power for good in my
hands, to live.

Calling the multitude together one morning I declared
that in the magnitude of my benevolence it was my purpose
to confer with them and listen to their grievances, if they
had any, against me, their most faithful friend, me who
had the right to drive them into exile but who suffered
them to remain, and blessed them by dwelling in the same
land, teaching them many things. "Why are you discontented? Why unhappy? The air is yours and the light;
I do not compel you to work in dungeons as I might by the
laws of God and sound political economy, nor underground;
I keep you at work from daybreak to dark because of my

loving solicitude for your morals; while you are working you cannot do wrong and your souls will be saved; dig my gold with a pure heart and take none of it, and I will bring you up in the fear of the Lord—and if you take it, in the fear of the Policeman; pray, when your hearts faint with labor, when your backs break, when your woolly brains throb with longing for the pastimes which to lead you into the green pastures I have compelled you to renounce; pray in fact all the time; when your stomachs are empty there is nothing so light and cheap and stimulating as prayer and you cannot overeat it; take no thought for the morrow, for if you work as hard as you should today there will be no tomorrow for you. I have come mainly to teach you the commercial possibilities of prayer: there is no grief in the savage breast but prayer will assuage it after death; no passion in the savage frame but prayer will extinguish it, with the help of Christian bullets if necessary; nothing which may be good for the savage but prayer will help you to do without it, for be sure that what you do not get by prayer you will not get in any other way. There is no toiler's rheumatism that prayer will not heal, no pain of body or spirit that prayer will not change into ravishing bliss if assisted by strong drink. Man was created an infinite sufferer purely to learn the puissance of prayer. This world is a sink of anguish from the cradle to the grave in order to teach people God's infinite love for them. The Devil, who will make man suffer a trifle more hereafter, therefore loves man a trifle more than God does."

Being now fairly launched in the tremulous luxury of preaching, in which I had been prophetically facile at the seminary, equaled only by several unprincipled theological scamps now in jail, and looking out upon the dusky throng of my parishioners, I beheld them with the tender emotions of a seer.

"What is misery? Whence is sorrow? Why do we feel

pain, when a blessed redeemer sits near us in the triumphant invisible, probably weeping? It is to learn that before the breath of prayer misery, pain and sorrow fade away like the light of a match in the blast of a storm. My hearers, if I seem to be a stern taskmaster it is to remind you of your father which is in heaven, if for your eternal good and the austere obligations of civilization I deprive you of every happiness you have known, faint not, be of good cheer, remember the enormous openings I make for you into the hereafter. There you can sit in idleness forever and thank God that you met me in time to learn the road to eternal life; there you can evolve, passing cheerfully up from one story of immaculate existence to another, never overworking, nor sweating, nor hungry, nor sick, nor betrayed, nor robbed, as you are here, having no master but the eternal God, and thrilling day and night, with the exquisite vibrancy of holy passion and illimitable love. For there you will never slumber or tire. Dearly beloved, I make you toil with no remission now that your eternal rest may be sweeter when you stumble home to the wormy grave; I blunt your feelings and beclod your intellects here to sharpen and polish them for the infinite feelings they are to feel when this finite vesture is laid aside and sick mortality fades into cured immortality; I buffet you now that the dear God may have many wounds to heal when you climb into the haven of his bosom, so that you may speedily learn his pitying fathomless tranquil grace and replenishing compassion. Be thankful if I put you to torture, cause you to work nights as well as days, mutilate you, tear mother from child and virtue from maid and heap all manner of blessed infamy upon you, in the name of our Heavenly Lord, rejoice and be exceeding glad, for I am his instrument appointed to break the manacles of flesh from your souls by dreadful scourgings of your bodies; I stop at nothing because somewhere you must experience burning cosmic wrath before you can endure super-cosmic light; I would like to append new faculties of tribulation to your earthly organs in order that your impending transfiguration might be more divine and my profits larger. And God forbid that you should resist, God forbid that you should be your own stumbling-blocks to perfection, welcome all afflictions, be humble, be submissive, be poor of spirit, beseech the bountiful Giver of afflictions for more, and trust my ingenuity to apply them in such a manner that you will be lacerated to your full measure of woe."

I fain would have continued speaking in this vein for a much longer time, for I felt myself wafted back to New York and suffused with the most enlightened emotions that a Christian can feel, but I perceived an insurrection brewing among the common people. At one corner of the congregation certain of the less worthy brethren were collecting stones of convenient dimensions to heave, and the malcontents seemed to be gaining converts to their nefarious defection from duty faster than I to the sublime truths of the noblest religion ever promulgated to the fallen, and hastily saying amen I inquired of Milto if the people had a complaint. Acting as their national spokesman the peerless chief arose and declared himself as follows:

"Preeminent Brain (which was the title they had conferred upon me against the dictates of my modesty), we are deeply sensible of the thousand blessings which you have brought to us from the sky and elsewhere, and we bow before the condescending sweetness of your virtues. Not the least of these imperishable gifts is your godlike eloquence, which we could listen to from the hour when first the ruddy glow of the time-keeper of heaven speckles our beautiful bodies until the flaming teeth of sacrificial hunger redden them for the last time, were it not that no god has yet endowed us with the angelic competence to live on melody alone. You have permitted us to enjoy for a

season the homes of our forefathers; you preserved our
lives, for if you had forced us to wander from our native
land into the night we must have starved or fallen before
the iniquitous hunger of wild beasts, or been consumed by
the vengeful prowess of competing cannibals in the pathless
brush; you have taught us industry, enabled us to sleep on
our poles, conferred upon us the adorable benefit of length-
ening them four times; you have been a great and powerful
promoter of education in our midst; you have established
free libraries with wealth our toil created; and you support
our lives by giving us work in the kindly vastitude of your
condescension—how was it that we ever lived before you
came? We do not speak of the presents, which are from
your sky-ruling brother-in-law*: but all these now seem as
nothing to us: we have observed your ravening fondness
for gold; we do not know what it is good for, or why you
want it; but seeing a god like you care for it with all the
focused fevers of his infinite undying soul, we infer that it
must be good for something, and you can't blame us for
wanting part of it, too."

"That you shall certainly have," I cried, feeling as one
restored from the dead. "We will begin at once."

CHAPTER XIV

I Pay Wages and Restore Happiness

I divided the output of the previous week into three
equal parts, replacing two of them in my oaken safe for
myself; the third I split equally, giving half to the god, in
a box, and portioning the other half to the King, great men,

---

*This was a favorite Rinyo idiom of flattery; the complemental curse
was "Brother-in-law of Lazuck," one of their Satans, in which they
were richer than ourselves by having several.

and people, in the manner and proportion employed by His Sceptred Justice in disbursing the brass roosters and beads. This was marvelously satisfactory to all, who could hardly believe their senses on seeing me part with so much. The conventicle was breaking up when I motioned the King to beat loudly on a gong, as the signal for them to resume their seats. I then addressed them.

"Heretofore I have permitted you to use the picks and shovels, pans and toothpicks taken from the caravan, without charge, and also that new four-fifths part of the poles which I affixed to their size. So long as our relation was one of pure affection without strict business rules, as it has been till now, my tender concern caused me to continue this loving laxity. Then you needed nothing, we were as one family, whatever was essential to your comfort and piety I furnished freely out of a full heart; you were my children; but now you have shown a revolting relish to sever these sweet spontaneous ties, to stand alone, to discard my throbbing solicitude; now you are to have a stated commercial share to gratify your foolish pride of independence, you have abrogated the reign of love, abjured the fond fellowship of fatherhood, and I shall be obliged to require payment for the use of the shovels and poles, for the scraps which your children and women collect for your food, and rent for the ground on which you sleep, which I find upon figuring will come to just the sum of gold that each individual has received."

These children of twilight nature were a fair minded people, not avidious of what was not their own, endowed with a rough intuitive perception of right and wrong, altho I had formerly thought otherwise. They saw that I was right, and everyone of them without compulsion or further persuasive eloquence, came forward and deposited the gold I had paid him in my box. I fastened down the lid of the receptacle of god's portion and my own with stout padlocks, and the meeting adjourned. It was the last trouble of the kind I had with these excellent Africans, true creatures of innate equity and light. It proved that ideas of justice will grow even in the bog of barbarism, let civilized psychologists say what they will. I had changed their economic system with a little speech, and now their happiness flowed on placidly again toward the silent ocean of the boundless beauty of holiness. They were just where they were before the economic change, so far as quantity of material goods counted, but the length of the moral stride they had compassed was prodigious. Before, they were minion children of feudal barbarity without a dollar in their pockets from week's end to end, now for a few minutes every Saturday afternoon they felt the glow of gold in their clothes, or, since they did not wear clothes, in their handkerchiefs, which I had taught them to use for cleanliness and culture. Charity had ceased, they now paid as they went, and no bill of shovel-rent was mounting up to mow at them in their dreams.

It was my rule to allow each one to hold his gold in the palm of his hand for five minutes, within a few inches of his eyes, looking steadily at it, before restoring it to my box, to deeply inculcate into him the sense and virtues of property. Holding it thus and knowing it to be his own, he imbibed the sentiment of ownership, he planted the fiery instinct that would grow and consume all its associates; it would be a yoke to harness him to the car of human toil; he would become blind to the pleasures of life and absorbed in its beautiful purpose, possession. This is making a savage truly become as a little child, born under the star of a dollar, feeding the nude little germ from the nursing-bottle of pious greed, giving him a weekly peep at our civilization's deadly grandeur through the sanctified lens of his personal abstinence, seating him on the stool of blistering hope in the torrid sun of a billionaire for the ratification of his own everlasting distress. Five minutes' weekly possession of a little gold I found to be quite long enough to give the transcendental motive of civilization firm root in the savage belly.

What an incredible folly it was, I often said to myself, that drove our excellent grandfathers to make slaves of their fellow beings in order to cudgel activity out of their skins, when a few grains of gold placed before their noses every week or month, and called theirs as long as you can hold your breath, is a salient sorcerer to conjure out their inward vitality in toil for the employing wizard who baptizes their concupiscent palms with the instantly evaporating magic. The heathen are as thirsty gulls as the Christian, the savage is as cheaply bought as the civilized; the will o' wisp specter of the eternal Have beckons and compels saint and sinner over the whole earth, if they have two legs, no tail, and are men, to flit about bleeding away their souls until they have poured the potent juices of their life into some magnet owner's wallet-skin, and have and are nothing. To become a rejected blood-sack for the accommodation of a repleted blood-sucker is the common ardor and glory of man. God be praised that he has given men this gentle proclivity. Who would build our palaces and crowd our armies to fight and die for the rich, without this far-sighted attribute of the multitude? Mind- and muscle-spoiling toil would not consecrate itself prostrate at the feet of cormorant idleness but for the deep sweet godlike emotion the toiler feels when he receives his weekly wages at six o'clock and pays them out for his weekly bills at seven, an imaginary lord of property one spangled hour.

So I mused, letting my mind run where it would without much rudder or destination, and one day gave my darling savages a little homily on the subject. It was at the noon hour and they had finished the dinner which their women brought to them in these days regularly on chips.

"Fellow manufacturers—for I must now call you by a

name which recognizes the dignity and equality of labor—
I rejoice in the manifestations of spiritual life that are beginning to advertise themselves on your persons. When I
came to your filthy hovels you were exceedingly gross and
fleshly and healthy, you are now hopefully thin and diseased; I like the appearance of those sores on your bodies,
which indicate that you are being chastened for divine ends;
emaciation is an excellent remedy for the sins of Adam;
while the body is luscious the mind seldom develops a proper
ethical system—at least one that will live after the author
is dead; savage profligacy is a foe to all missionary movements; many have lost their lives in attempting to rear
families with a high standard of comfort while working
for the Master of the Vineyard under the direction of His
vice masters; neglect your children and the Lord will take
them up; man should study the beasts, who die heroically
mute; the fear of the Lord and the fat of the land are
never found in the same company; if Blessed are the peacemakers, more blessed are they who create strife, that the
peacemakers may have a job and obtain their reward; the
rich man cannot go through the eye of a needle nor enter
the kingdom of heaven, therefore toil for your enemies to
make them rich and keep them out of heaven; you will have
plenty Above if they remain Below, not otherwise;—I am
willing to be regarded as an enemy of all mankind, if they
will try to keep me out of heaven.

"I have noticed some of you conning manuals of hygiene;
put them aside, health is inimical to holiness; the healthy
man loves life, therefore go work in a factory and you will
soon see God; set not your affections on the things of this
world, for none of them belong to you; give all that thou
hast to the rich, for if you do not they will soon take it
away from you; praise God for suffering and disease, those
beautiful possessions of the poor, out of which the worms
of saintly sorrow that refine and devour the soul grow;

blessed are the seeds of consumption, for like our rich they blossom into great monopolists of life; if you would awaken people to the conviction of sin and the melancholy certainty of religion, destroy their health—though to call their children from the slums below to the palaces above may answer in the poorest families; I shall apply these ideas with devotion to you.

"These are general remarks, preparatory to a few hortatory observations on the value of money. The value of money consists in saving it. For five minutes every week you are rich; hoard your possessions carefully during that time, for the state of your mind is then no less exalted than the billionaire's, who has more and keeps it longer; it is the quality of sentiment, not the quantity of money, that unites men; he whose quantity of profit is a cent a year may have the same quality of sentiment as that brother whose annual profit is a hundred millions, if he is a Christian Scientist. Praised be God for the eruption of Christian Science and Buddhism, for those whom sweet Christianity does not make contented with misery and millionaries these opium-theologies will; preserve the stench and horrors of this world that the mind may increase in agility by denying them; a steak in the millionaire's stomach and the million dollars in his pocket are really in yours if you can piously think so; but what of the millionaire's hunger and empty pocket when you have thought his food and money out of him into yourself? He must think them back;—in this wise one million dollars and a single tenderloin steak may be thought around the world through every pocket and stomach, and all be rich and fed. This is the safest way to steal, as well as enabling the rich by eating everything there is to bless the poor.

"Both you and I are capitalists in our hearts, altho there is a small discrepancy in the material amounts we have; we both want more, and therefore our souls rattle together in the unison of speculative similitude. Remember the sacredness of property and be not envious of a fellow capitalist because he has more than you; if you save the memories of the gold that you so fondly caress on pay-days and put them in the savings bank you may sometime be as rich in memories as I am in realities. By an inscrutable dispensation of God which it were profane to inspect—since it was invented and given to the human race by brutally ignorant ancient savages and is therefore holy—a somewhat larger share of gold falls to me than to you; that is nothing so long as you have *some*; if you were wholly deprived, it would be your pious duty to create a disturbance, and I should lead you in an attack upon defunct tyrants, feudal systems, and other dead things, to establish your inalienable right to a few substanceless ghosts of the good things of this world. We should find the tyrants in the North Pole and the feudal systems in the past ages, and should go forth in a blithering fury, with flags and lurid patriotism and a conquering shout, to exterminate both. (Most of you would not come back. You would leave your patriotism and yourselves to parch by the side of the prehistoric mummies you had slaughtered.) But now you have all the good things possible to a free people, and crusades and purgative French Revolutions are needless, for gold inundates your palms for five long thronging minutes a week.

"I discovered this darling substance, I molded the plan which made these picks and shovels ours, and, you being only physical instruments of my will in the transaction, all we get becomes mine. God works in these peculiar ways, perhaps to amuse himself, and certainly to bring us all to a state of repentance: he makes us all repent that he exists. Only the work of the scheming mind deserves reward. You must see that God's will is done, for the bible shows that He easily becomes ugly. Let nothing tempt you to take my gold, to preserve which the ten commandments were written; should you take it you would destroy your right to possess your gold for five minutes, when you would have nothing and would sink back into the abject misery where I found you, without sores, God, the hope of an early death, and an immortal life of unconsciousness. If you invade my property right you invade your own. I charge you, brethren, by your faith in the Most High, of whom I will tell you more when business slackens, uphold the glorious privilege of money which now for the first time in your history blackens your horoscope."

My sweetly reasonable words sank deep into their dark diaphrams. At the end of every week I delivered over their share of their week's work, and to the King and the great ones their manyfold larger share for doing nothing, which with truthful honesty and blushing pleasure they all returned to my strong box in payment for my generous loan of the shovels and poles. I pointed out that my services as director and overseer of the digging were of high commercial value but that I threw them in as a free gift, and I think this unexpected munificence brought me more pure love from their guileless bosoms than even my sermon on economic principles. Nevertheless I was cautious to anchor them with another fundamental impulse to the rock of gain; I contracted that if they worked faithfully and made no trouble I would raise their salaries by adding one minute every three months to the time of their holding the gold.

CHAPTER XV

SOME SUPERFLUOUS RINYOS

There were unfortunately not enough picks, shovels and other implements to supply all the men with tools, and this threw me into a distressing perplexity. Before I began to pay wages I had no objection to the surplus individuals who were without tools scratching around with their finger-nails and getting out what gold they could. They obtained quite enough to pay handsomely for their keep, and as I did not allow them to use it for that purpose but appropriated it to myself their toil supplied me with a respectable yield, tho nothing for me to care much about compared with the rest. However, I saw no reason, moral or material, why they should not be permitted to keep at it, with the privilege of eating the bits that their women collected for their food by night. It was not that they had any right to live under these circumstances, but as they cost me nothing, besides being the source of considerable revenue in the aggregate, my good nature and Christian theology ruled in their favor. Let them potter along, reflected I magnanimously, they are probably more cheerful alive than dead, and Africa is an out-of-the-way place where the bad example of their limited usefulness to me cannot demoralize the white man.

But this generously negligent attitude could not continue after the short-sighted batrachians had begun to exact wages of me. My duty to their brethren with the shovels who were turning out the enormous profits I wanted would not endure this. To pay equal wages to these two sets of men when one of them produced so much and the other so little, would be disgracefully unjust and had only to be thought of to be rejected, as not only basely unfair to me but wickedly so to those Rinyos whose use of shovels and picks enabled them to be the large producers.

It was very easy with a little figuring to decide what just wages for the toolless would be. To be strictly fair I measured the sum of gold secured by a certain number of the tool-workers, and by the same number destitute of the implements, and found the former to be fifty times more a day, so that by irreproachable economic and Christian principles and arithmetic the wages of the toolless should be a fiftieth part of those paid to the rest.

The tool-users' wages, as I explained before, just paid for the use of the tools, for the rent of the holes in the rocks in which they slept when it rained, for the rent of the ground they slept on when it did not rain, and finally for the fragments of food collected by their children and wives in the night. A fiftieth part of these wages, to which the toolless by digging gold with their fingers and toes were entitled, would therefore pay for a hole one-fiftieth large enough to sleep in, which would by no means cover one of their feet, for only the same fraction of ground space for them to lie down on, so that they would have to sleep standing up, and for only a fiftieth part of the food necessary to sustain life. I was willing to pay them this amount of wages, but what was the use? Such wages would only yield them a fiftieth of the strength after a few days, so that the product of their work would drop to practically zero. Besides, since, when earning no more than that, they would soon die, it was better to cut the agony short and discharge them at once and altogether, when death would sooner overtake and tenderly release them. One can escape from some things, but never from mathematics, so I arrived with hopeless certainty at the afflicting conclusion that there was no way for these superfluous people to live.

At this debilitating discovery, as I need not inform you, my sensitive heart prompted me to shed streams of inconsolable tears, and I turned the subject over in my mind a thousand times in the longing to discern some way of evading the rigid decrees of structural cosmic righteousness by which to prolong their lives. I reasoned thus in the vain endeavor to find a solution:

Food for them to live on is plentiful and it costs me nothing. I cannot eat it, nor can I permit the whole Rinyo tribe to do so, to whom I already allow all that they earn.

Since these toolless workers do not net me a large profit,
why should I not free them entirely from laboring for my
gain and give them liberty to spend their time gathering
their own food?

Against these propositions the whole integrity and antiquity of my ape-engendered intellect, supported by the
laws of a still more antiquated Divine Reason by which I
was illumined, of course cried out. I feared also that the
unfortunates might see this point, too, and level it at me.
The answer ought assuredly to be very evident to an honest
pagan, or to one duly humiliated by religion. If, ran my
ruminations, I liberated the resources of life and allowed
these five hundred shovelless superfluities to collect their
food directly, exempted from toil for me, they would have
to work but a little of the time to gain more and better food
than the gold-gatherers enjoyed, who worked terrifically
the entire day. Any one can see the direful injustice of
this to the gatherers, who, rather than less, deserved the
greater reward, because of their shining usefulness in increasing my wealth. Apart from this unthinkable injustice
it would create a dangerous and explosive jealousy, for the
diggers with tools, seeing the others getting a very good
living without working for me, and working only very moderately for themselves, would begin to ask why they should
work fearfully hard for my benefit, for the reward of an
exceedingly bad living. Being savages brilliantly endowed
with a stupid inability to grasp civilized perceptions, it
would be very hard to make them comprehend why.

Policy, no less than science and righteousness, demanded
therefore that the superfluous Rinyos should die. It did
cross my mind that I might suffer these needless wights
to take the place of some of the others part of the time,
during which they should use the shovels and picks while
the others were at rest, but I expelled the notion instantly
as dangerous to the morals of the workers. Idleness is the

worst foe of a working class. Workingmen rot morally if permitted time to think. It also gives them an opportunity to learn the pleasures of other things besides labor, which they have no right to know, since it robs their employer of some of their working strength.

I now prepared to convey my decision to the tribe as affectionately as I could, and I called Milto to me to play his part.

"Let us bring in the clergy," said I, "there is nothing that can cause men to starve with such vivid satisfaction as religion."

King Milto thereupon ordered his First Official Hypocrite and all the subordinate Idol-Trainers into our presence, when he commanded them to employ their most beatified and serpentine arguments to convert the superfluous Rinyos to a conviction of the public necessity of their death, and promised to raise the salaries of the clergymen if their cunning prevailed. By my permission, in fact, he assured them that a hundredth part of the food consumed by these surplus persons should, if their religion did its duty, be divided among the clergy after the surplus had ceased to eat, were dead, and redeemed.

I think the promise of a thousandth would have sufficed, for the clergy squirmed gleefully at the offer and began inventing nebulous reasons on the spot why the various gods they did business with required the immediate presence in Eternal Gladness of the wasted devils I wanted to dispatch. When you remember that a strict Rinyo article of faith was that all their gods were considered dead as a measure of public safety, that these dead creatures should have exercised a wish is quite African in its touching mysticism.

The formal discharge of the superfluous, into which I infused some ceremony for general unction, was rather a shock to the discharged, who knew it meant death, and they had the impoliteness to come in a body and disturb a siesta that I was taking at home to recuperate from the sorrow I felt for their fate. Their pleadings bored me, it was quite improper of them to interrupt my rest when I had already wept and prayed for them; but I let them jabber awhile for the sake of free speech, and when I could waste no more time with them I turned them out of doors forcibly but without anger, advising them to go into the woods and eat each other one by one, drawing lots who should go next, as the pleasantest way to terminate their existence.

"And," said I in parting, "it will help you very much if you accept Christianity. God is working out a great plan which I have considered and approved, of which your coming starvation through a dearth of shovels is a feature. Note the nicety of universal intention; the scarcity of shovels in that caravan was a very vital item in the infinite scheme. The plan of the universe may be rasping to creatures of your degraded dimensions, whose principal function, like that of the worm, is to be trampled on by the plan as it proceeds, yet I assure you that your being trampled on is what provides the meaning and pleasure of the plan. The Super-Power gave you capacity to feel for the pleasure of seeing you suffer. But being walked on by the universe never hurts Christians, for they are trained to enjoy it. They are grateful to the universe for crushing them. Of course, tho, if you embrace Christianity you will never see your ancestors again for they died in sin and are damned."

I hoped I had seen the last of them, and it seemed that such was the case. They disappeared and all was quiet for some time.

CHAPTER XVI

THE TERROR

Things went so well now that occasionally I appointed a state holiday for the transaction of such public business by the King as might have fallen into arrears through his assiduity in my service. He usually had a few subjects whom he desired to execute and I did not feel it to be good statecraft to have such punctual duties much delayed.

On one of these holidays about two months after the vanishment of the superfluous Rinyos I was sauntering over the metropolis delighting in the curious sights, and happened to be near the capitol building, when a disturbance in its vicinity caused me to hasten my steps toward that stately edifice, which was built of green mud. Something of unusual and terrible import was stirring. Fully two thousand of the hugest giants of the Kingdom, whom I recognized as the State Police from a great circular piece of bark stuck upon their breasts with gum as their official badge, all armed with the massive truncheons of their trade, were collected in a threatening attitude before the State entrance, while a mighty throng of spectators were assembled at a respectful distance awaiting some event with the deepest expectancy.

This was a remarkable proceeding, awakening in me the gruesome suspicion that the King might have conceived the pestilent project of rebelling against my yoke, in which event there was no time to lose. Forcing my way through the crowd of passive observers I advanced with stern outward composure and quivering interior toward the heavy cordon of guards at the palace portals. No sooner did they see and recognize me advancing alone across the opening than with a splitting scream of delight every one of the two thousand policemen fell down backwards with arms and legs rising parallel and perpendicular into the air, and remained there stark and silent awaiting my orders. Much relieved by this acclamation of allegiance, tho yet more mystified, I commanded them to stand, after my passage, and to resume their clubs, which they had dropped as they gyrated themselves, and strode across their rigid forms into the lofty vestibule, where I entered the royal tub and was drawn up to the King's private reception room.

The effulgent monarch was at one of the front windows of the executive chamber as I entered, peering down into the park below from behind an enormous snake-skin curtain which concealed him from view, and he was so gript by terror that he would have collapsed if four royal eunuchs had not supported him on each side, somewhat unsteadily however, for they danced about hysterically, bumping their demented heads now into each other and now into the sacred substance of the King.

When Milto saw me he tried to speak but could scarcely do so coherently.

"They come!" shuddered he, dropping the curtain and covering his face with his hands.

"Who come?" queried I. "What is this deuced ruction about?"

The sublime King could not reply, because his tongue refused to move; he could only point feebly out of the window.

"The malcontents, Great Savior," whispered one of the royal eunuchs.

At this I hastily tore the curtain aside and beheld a sight that would have petrified the bravest heart, particularly if clad in authority. A strange and terrifying object was proceeding toward the stately entrance of woven swamp-grass and sun-baked clay over which the two thousand policemen stood guard. I could not at first distinguish its character, tho as it squirmed forward I concluded it to be a savage monster of colossal magnitude and a species unknown to me which the people dared not attack. Just then Milto recovered himself sufficiently to issue a hurry order to one of the eunuchs that the policemen below should bellow violently to frighten the invader away. In a few moments the building shook with the frightful roars produced by the guard, who rendered the noise more horrible by thumping on the resonant earth with their clubs.

All this din had no effect, for the leviathan came on undismayed. A few more minutes of shattering suspense followed, when it reached a point where I could decipher its structure. It was a compact body of emaciated men, who sustained themselves on their feet by leaning together in a mass, the tottering weight of one side of the group propping up the other side, as two men tipping with drink support themselves by embracing each other when either alone would fall. Not much but bones and facial expression remained of these wasted beings, while as to strength they retained none, or barely enough to stagger slowly forward. In number they were about four hundred and fifty altogether.

"Have they smallpox, cholera, or what, that they frighten everybody so?" I demanded, hoping the King might have recovered the power of a few syllables from his general paralysis.

"Far worse," twitched he, his sublime teeth masticating themselves with the force of a mill, "it is Hunger! They are the superfluous population that you cast out, returning for vengeance."

I now saw there was much to fear, and I felt a sickening dread of what might overtake me because these miserable beasts did not acknowledge the principles of Wall Street and God and die as directed. The peppery spectacle of such shredded remains of men was liable to inflame the whole population, except of course the great, who were above it. An African inflammation, lacking the cooling aperient of culture, may forget its manners. A hungry man in a sedentary city soaked in the slime of civilized law may die on a park bench at 3 A. M., crustless, when an active African surcharged with the glowing memories of fight and slaughter may turn with contempt of court upon his lawful starver and kill him. In that hour of solemn crisis I would have given the Supreme Judges of the United States ten percent of my plunder could I have had their talented aid in ripening the illegal tissues of the children of primal falsehood about me. As I looked into their simple perceptions I saw down the windows of hell. I find I can always tie up an evolved nature in the loose threads of its own development, but the simple natures just born out of the primordial are cruel obstacles. They see and cannot think; the culture-coated think and cannot see. And they hit back. I hate a simple nature that hits back. The gaudiest triumph of civilization is that before a man can hit back by law he is dead. Were I going to Africa for gold again I should send $50,000,000 ahead to generate a university to prepare the inky souls for my coming. They would then starve with a scientific comprehension of their duty to do so.

Now every chuckle-headed Rinyo in the diocese knew that there was food in prodigious plenty all about, with no reason comprehensible to common sense why these shrunken starvelings should not eat it. The savage has no sense of humor and that places the Christian, who conducts his dealings with comical Christian cunning and playfulness, at a great disadvantage when alone among savages. I had several times noticed a savage tendency to take the Christian joke of starvation too seriously and it worried me now.

The starvers had by this time reached the lower door so that I had no time to meditate further. Milto was on his knees begging me piteously to save him, his vast frame cracking with tremors; the eight royal eunuchs, the King's seven private secretaries, and his Chief of Police had been lying on the floor ten minutes in a dead faint while the above reflections were occupying my mind. The royal valor was manifest over the cowardice of these caitiffs, for the King did not faint and had sufficient presence of mind to embrace my knees and repeatedly implore me convulsively to save his life and throne, with a voice suffocating with sobs.

"Now, Milto," I said, "do as I tell you and all will be well"—tho I was not so sure of it. "Calm your fears, dry your tears, receive these dying emaciants with the mien of a sovereign, and try your best to hide from them and the populace that you are in mortal fear for your life. Quake as it were haughtily to deceive them."

"Oh! Oh!" wailed His Sublimity, "go down and meet them for me, you have the armor of a thousand theories in your breast and I am naked."

"No, my dear boy," I answered, "we must use finesse. The time has come for stratagem, and I will stand behind you with all the theories named. Listen to my instructions. Receive them with deep sympathy, assure them that you feel for them, promise all the help in your power, declare with blinks of sorrow that you will carefully examine the laws on the subject of allowing surplus men to eat surplus food, point out with gulps of woe that the Rinyo Constitution stands in the way of your doing anything for them that you do not want to do, and that our Congress of Ancient Quacks prohibits everything else; be solemn, majestic and slippery: then come away and we will kill them off one by one by delays. The imbecile multitude will think we mean what we say, and if we can secretly tempt the starvers to steal a few vacant bones or a pig's tail, or to break into some butcher's cave, or put a stone through a plate glass window, or to make a little noise, we can instigate the common people to pounce on and slaughter them."

This program acted magically on Milto, and he hastened to execute it by a conference with the skeletons, with the wise foresight however of throwing over his head and body a gigantic lion-skin with the teeth ominously exposed, and by placing himself in the center of a human circle composed of his bark-badged club-swingers fifty deep, who formed a compact mass of protection around him so that he felt partially safe.

I awaited the end of the conference with concern, knowing that my career was in the balance. If these scurvy vagrants refused to die in an orderly and constitutional manner, I should be at my wit's end to know what to do about it, for the light of human experience shone no farther. The civilized surplus always die when commanded to do so to vindicate the perfection of human society—what should I do if the sodden savage shied at the privilege?

The King returned chapfallen and pallid, showing that he had failed, and he brought me the dying men's ultimatum. They declared they would not stir from the public place unless food were supplied; they insisted on seeing me immediately where they were; and they required that I should make them a provision of food for the future, either with work or without it.

The memorial ended with these atrocious words:

"You told us that we were out of work because we were not Christians, that if we believed on your god Christ he would provide for us, that no true believer on him was ever in want. So we went home and believed; we became Christians and implored his help; we went on believing and expecting with all the belief and expectation in us for two months; fifty of us died of that belief and the rest of us have hardly body enough left for a belief to cling to; no help came, and we saw that all of us would die if we continued to be Christians and that your Christianity was a cheat; nearly dead tho we are, every one of us is completely cured of your Christ-God disease. We know by trial that no god helps the needy, and we do not believe there is a god. You have babbled of god to us to humbug us into obedience."

Shocked and grieved at this flippant blasphemy I tore this part of the document to pieces that it might not fall into the hands of other heathen to endanger their salvation. Christianity never failed to reconcile civilized workingmen to starvation, and it wrung my heart to find it shaky for doing as much for the savage.

Affairs in the street at this instant reached a very critical stage indeed. Attracted by the unusual occurrence increasing crowds had collected, among whom, aided by some flashing Rinyoese profanity, the story of their comrades' starvation caused by my refusal to give them work was being bandied about. Their passions, too, were beginning to sizzle to such a degree that unless I could soothe them with a few precious insights I was likely soon to be trampled into the pavement.

Sustained by truth I went out resolutely to face them. They were abashed by my presence and the fierce shout they tried to raise died away miserably on their quavering lips, but the spokesman of the starvers, a very fiend in appearance from long fasting and the recent ravages of atheism, delivered himself thus, very curtly and uncouthly, with none of the titles of admiration which, while thoroughly despising, I detected to have a euphonious lilt for the ear:

"Allow us to use some of the shovels and picks part of the time, thereby enabling us to earn food and giving the relieved workers periods of rest to gather strength for harder work when they resume their tools. Your income can hardly be less from this plan, for both groups, being fresher, will do more while they work. But if it is less, we live; and we consider our lives more valuable than your income."

"My pretty fellow," cried I, "—I hesitate to call you a ghostly dunce for fear of wounding your emaciated sensibilities—*you* are not the ones to decide what your life is worth, it has long since been settled throughout the world that that is the business of the man who hires you. You positively seem to have no more comprehension of business principles than an angel. I degrade business principles by talking with you, but I will do so since you are only a heathen African. Pray, why should I support two lots of men when one lot can do the work? Wouldn't the food of the second lot be a useless waste? What business is it of mine what becomes of that second lot of workers? I am only called on to support those I have work for."

"Glorified One," stammered he, humbled by my merciless logic, "it is rumored that you are the supported one, supported by these workers. If they are willing to support you, does it concern you how many of them join to do it? If a thousand of them can sustain you more easily than five hundred, and all the thousand get a living for themselves too, are you not satisfied?"

"By no means," I roared, "for I can allow only that number to support me from whom I can derive the best support and extract the most wealth besides. This is the Science of Being Supported, popularly called Political Economy because politics are always used to economize the food of the workers, and a supported person would be a baboon indeed if he allowed his supporters to dissipate on their own stomachs wealth he might have. Not only a baboon but one quite ripe for a lunacy commission."

I felt his pulse and continued:

"Be honest with yourself a minute, for you will soon be at the mercy of One Who Abominates Foolish Thinking And Punishes Fools: if these micro-minded Rinyos were suffered to connect the idea of rights to anything at all with their own stomachs, where would it end? Wouldn't every roaring rogue of them soon be saying that he had a right to as much food and as much gold as I?"

Thereupon the cantankerous beast let himself out in the following farrago:

"We claim the right to have work wherewith to earn our food. Food is abundant. We declare the Law of Food to be that every one has a just right to a share of food equal to that of every other person, *if he is willing to work,* whether you grant him work or not. Wherefore we have made up our minds to take food from you or any one who has it if you refuse us work."

I gasped as the dying man hysterically ejaculated this nauseous drivel. "Bosh" was on the end of my tongue but I retained it. The knave was ages ahead of his time, and by blurting out the naked truth like that had certainly lost the sympathy of the whole tribe; while as for taking food from anybody, his tottering tissues could not have done so from a butterfly.

"You are an anarchist," said I in a very loud voice. "You deserve nothing after venting such inflammatory drool; whether you receive anything shall be left to the people,"—whereupon I repeated his insolent speech to the assemblage.

How could the situation have shaped itself more merrily to my purpose? This man had proclaimed his right to take food from us all: now it happened that all the people had far less than enough, and if the smallest quantity were taken from them they would suffer; I, however, had a great plethora and could feed the entire nation well without depriving myself. But just here was the snare in which I caught them: if the people admitted the starving man's right to take food from me who would not miss it, they seemed to admit also his right to seize food from them, who would miss it frightfully—so they were all much angered at the idea of his taking it from anyone, and were fiercely incensed against the spokesman, at whom they cried, "Down with the anarchist!" (without knowing what it meant). "Death to him!" which neatly saved me.

So in excellent spirits I delivered the outwitted spokesman over to them, to be dragged off to a high eminence and pitched down upon the jagged rocks below, to bleach there until the centuries should catch up with him. It was better for him to be dead, for, born so long ahead of his time, no one could understand him, and loveless and mateless he was destined to wander the bleak world alone. I did him a kindness to chuck him out of it.

CHAPTER XVII

Better Than Bullets

After this little comedy it flashed into my mind how to deal with the survivors.

"Work," observed I caressingly, waving the populace to close about me in an open-mouthed human wall far-stretching and greedy for knowledge, "is no man's right, as the departed fanatic who was just with us probably now suspects. The proof of this virtuous universal law is Nature's unfailing association of believers in the right to work, with jagged rocks, police clubs, prison cells, guillotines, gibbets, gatling guns and other visible manifestations of nature's convictions. These things always follow an advanced man as burns follow fire, revealing nature's design that we should keep enlightened thoughts out of our heads, in which I agree with nature. If every man had a right to work, coupled with suitable pay for it, we should be unable to hold the poor in their place; no man could get rich by

keeping others poor, for as no workers would be out of
work, no employer could force down general wages by
threatening to hire the workless in place of his workers
at less pay."

"Tremendous!" acclaimed the populace; "there *must* be
men out of jobs, we see it now, dear Master; that's one of
the prices we pay for having you, and we know very well
that if you didn't pay us wages we should all die."

"That you would," echoed I, "speedily."

"But how are you going to satisfy the workless with their
situation?" asked they, "a situation so necessary to your
wealth and our lamentable want?"

"That's easy too," affirmed I, "with a little reasoning.
And now since your hearts are again juicy with love, and
your minds duly sensitive to the iniquity of justice, I will
tell you how.

"You knew not the true aim of life and had experienced
neither happiness nor virtue before I came. I taught you
that the noblest aim of being is to make some one else rich;
here, I am the one; it is by laboring for that sanctified end
that you become happy and virtuous. Otherwise your joy
is froth and your goodness crime, and I might say your
whole life is as vain as a boil. Is this clear?"

"And sparkling as wine," they boomed.

"Now there is one very common mistake made by men
in passing up into these alpine theories of rarified happiness
and I fear you are making it. You seem to think, as many
uncultured people before you have thought, that life is
necessary to happiness—which is a chaotic error that some
workingmen are especially addicted to. Take my word for
it, you can be just as happy dead as alive, and happier if
your religion does not leak, for religion notifies us that the
best happiness is kept in a refrigerator in the sky awaiting
the arrival of our corpses. Dear souls, as a common man's
daily virtue consists in going without what he needs, his

supreme virtue lies in going without life for his betters'
sake, which we often remind him of by taking it away from
him. We find that death trains him to enjoy being dead;
he develops an instinct for staying dead. These combina-
tions of bones that are clamoring for food there, are blind
to the happiness they enjoy in being permitted to die for a
great cause. As I remarked, I am that cause.

"Now let us scientifically examine the absurdity of their
rebelling against such a mission. The science of it, beloved
children, is as follows:

"When a system of society is changed, those who cannot
fit in ought to be very much disgusted with themselves to
go on living in everybody's way, selfish hindrances to the
happiness of the new system.

"There is science enunciated in ultimates. Reason here
reaches the philosophical union of oneness and circumference; science achieves the Absolute, skins it, stuffs it, and
rests in it forever.

"From the above mighty induction an inference no less
than this is deduced: Civilization joins with religion in
the transcendent postulate that a workingman's life is worthless, and its one redeeming action death, when it pleases
the rich."

In reverence for science I paused and mopped my brow;
the shoals of Rinyos who had pursued my keen synthesis
with lurid delight trumpeted assent.

"However, I shall not insist on the happiness of these
murky-minded tramps who spurn the matchless pleasures
of death. It shall depend on you. I can give them no
work, because I will not be unjust to you. Were I to deprive you occasionally of the picks and shovels for their
use for a time, you could not earn enough to live in the
happy state of semi-starvation to which I have assigned
you. I can *give* them no food, for, whatever crimes may
gibber at my door, I refuse to commit that most execrable
one of pauperizing the paupers.

"But I will not force death on them. I grant you all permission to give them a remnant of your lean victuals— of which you already have far from enough—if you desire to do so in defiance of the law I shall make that they must not ask for it, disregarding which will entail a hundred lashes and jail on the culprit."

I held up my hand to check the volcanic applause elicited by this generosity and continued: "I do this to teach you christian charity, your poverty of which appals me. The foundation of christian charity is that you shall allow me to take the larger part of everything in order to make a handsome host of sufferers for you to help. If I did not seize everything there would be no sufferers and no opportunity for charity, when christianity would die of having nothing to do, so that the existence of Christianity rests on me. You see, I am a divine institution. It pleases Buzzrack to have sufferers helped, but not much helped, for people think of Buzzrack only when they are suffering; and thinking of Buzzrack is religion. If helped a little they imagine that Buzzrack is the helper, and, pleading for more help, they keep him in mind. Therefore the greatest benefactor of mankind, and Buzzrack's best friend, is he who creates sufferers. I came here largely for that purpose. It would be wrong for me to assist these evanescent human skin-sacks, for that would take away the privilege of doing so from you: the blessing comes only when those who have next to nothing help those who have nothing.

"But here is a point that will be of service to the brighter intellects: if any of you by the hypnotic action of eloquence upon your neighbor's emotions, or by the promise that he will receive a duplex heavenly reward, can induce him to give these stalwart beggars twice his share, you need give nothing yourself."

The crowd of potential rioters dispersed, engrossed in

discussion of the new ideas I had given them, each trying to induce the man at his elbow to present the surplus starvers with a porcupine's neck, a chicken's bill, an eagle's claw, or some other morsel of delicacy to eat, so that he might not have to give anything himself, meanwhile leaving the dying ghosts in the square quite unattended, with nothing but a contribution of general human kindness cut in thin slices to subsist on. Everybody looked upon these evaporating paupers as persons to escape giving anything to, while getting the credit on earth and in heaven of having generously supplied their wants, which was the covert design I had had in addressing them.

Several of the workless in fact now died on the ground before my eyes, upon whose shadowy incarnations the policemen swiftly jumped to eat the remains raw, but they could find no vestige of flesh anywhere on the delinquent frames to console their teeth. They would probably all have died, being too weak to get home, if a new illumination had not possessed me. I ordered a couple of cans of dishwater and garbage from the nearest hotel and issued permission to the sufferers to eat.

"The State is merciful," commented I, "and its bowels of compassion cannot allow you to die yet. Come around to the mines tomorrow and I think I can still make you useful."

They came as ordered, their wives and children carrying the weakest of them. Choosing a broad-topped boulder where the sun beat spitefully down, so large that they could all group in a huddle on its crest, "Stand there," said I, "before the eyes of the rest while they work: it will show them what a privilege they enjoy in having work; for if I did not furnish them work they would be where you are. You are an object-lesson of my sleepless kindness to your companions, whom I graciously permit to toil and make me a multi-billionaire. When they see your ghastly plight they will adore me as the giver of their happiness, and will toil harder lest I should take away their job and reduce them to what you are."

The starvers thanked me with tears and happy cries for making them useful again and giving them a cause to exist, if only as mere skin, also inquiring, very decently, how they were to live while they carried on this occupation.

"Let me consider," answered I, musing. "You may beg what you can get of the workers if you will do it on the sly. If you are seen begging I shall have to let you do time in jail for six months and feed you on 'a common wingless parasitic insect, with a flat body, and short legs furnished with claws,' which you will be authorized to gather from the jail walls and your own personalities. It will be an appetizing contest to see which consumes the other first. I inflict this punishment because if the workers are bitten by the fancy that they can live well like you by begging they will all drop work and turn beggars too, which, between you and me as honest men, I would do if I were in their places rather than toil my head off for somebody else as they are doing."

They agreed to this and cheerfully applied themselves to their new profession, tho thinking their wage a little slim. At this juncture I assembled the workers in a separate place alone to give them a private tip to this effect:

"These fellows," explained I, "who profess they cannot get work and are certain to beg for your help, are really a pack of lazy liars that do not want work and would not do a stroke if they could get it; they would dodge a job if they thought it liable to hit them; you can see this by the size and rectitude of their exhibited bones, of which I never saw finer living specimens uncovered. Work is running after them all the time and they are running faster to get away from it, in spite of the fact that their weak-

ness is such that they can just walk. When these merry
hoboes solicit alms remember that most of them are impos-
tors and don't be taken in. As there may be a few deserving ones among them you can give a small dole here and
there, but with discrimination, first dissecting their stomachs
to corroborate their statements if possible."

I nevertheless made my hearers clearly comprehend that
there were many more workers than were needed, to hinder
them from demanding an enlargement of their pay. Nor
did I try to reconcile this assertion with the one that the
starving surplus were idle because they were lazy, and that
they could work if they wished—there was no need of
reconciling them. The barbaric black mind prefers its ideas
loose and roving, and is so roomy that mutually slaughtering notions can swim around in it without finding each
other. The white mind is not like this.

I had now completely steeled the people against these
expiring wrecks, so that never again could there be danger
of a rising in their behalf. It is truly wonderful what our
Western charitable ideas will do when sagaciously stacked.
They coil about and prostrate the savage intellect like chlor-
oform. It is a mistake to suppose that whiskey and the
christian venereal diseases are the best means for exterminating savages: whiskey and christian charity administered by upright minds are far more efficient. I can vouch
for this from my own success. I even got along perfectly
without the whiskey, but I have a better grasp of christian
ideas than most. To deal correctly with idolators the
choicest thoughts of our humanitarian thinkers are better
than the choicest soft-nosed bullets. Wherever bullets are
resorted to I consider that brains and christian principles
are wanting. But where brains and character are absent,
as they are from most civilizers, I advise the use of bullets
that spread as they go in. 'They have an impact ball and
small air chamber inserted in the point, making the expan-

sion positive. They are quite different from the usual
"soft-nosed" or mushrooming type of bullet. The ball acts
as a wedge with scientific accuracy and compels the metal
jacket to expand the instant it strikes a soft tissue. It tears
a large wound, which is sufficient to bring down the heathen
by blood loss alone.' But the moral objection to them is
that while they open ample holes for the soul to escape
they carry no attachment for saving that eternal entity on
its way out. A text of scripture might be packed in each
bullet but for the expense. These bullets act more con-
cisely than grog and I concede are nearly as infallible as
the christian harem diseases. Yet they are all very much
like combing the hair with a hayrake, compared with the
scientific transports I feel from watching my civilized doctrinal poisons extirpate the savages' various powers while
still permitting their desouled bodies to walk about alive.

My victory in the instance just cited was complete. At
the same time, for the purpose of soaking the superfluous
Rinyos with a reverence for the State embodied in me, I
had the garbage and dishwater hauled up to their rock
every third day. There was soon a vile epidemic among
them which carried off three hundred. I had now the
choice of saving the garbage to enrich the soil of Africa or
of creating another batch of superfluous appetites to take
their places, nor did I hesitate. I had learned that the
horrible presence of these unused men as an overhanging
threat to the rest made all the latter work as if the devil
were pronging them, from dread of getting there themselves; so when the three hundred died I discharged three
hundred more into idleness, to go upon the loathsome rock
and take their turn with the plague, giving as a reason for
doing so that the picks and shovels were wearing out too
fast.

Tho the pest continued its distressing business on the
rock I had no fear of the contagion reaching me, since I

lived well and maintained excellently virtuous habits. The
appearance of consumption in a very expeditious form
among the workers displeased me more, because a general
depopulation of the realm would shrivel my income. Consumption is a well-known moral agency needing no word
of praise. It is the safest adjunct of christianity for de-
populating the unnecessary poor, as our capable tenements
in my dear American fatherland show.

Prosperity was now incarnate. I found that ghastly
rock, the hideous perch of the rotting surplus workers,
more potent as a power for good than a thousand whipping
posts could ever have been for the purification of the slave.

CHAPTER XVIII

RINYO MARRIAGE

As time sped the King and his subjects, besides their
interesting and instructive crop of new diseases which I
studied closely, taking voluminous notes for the benefit of
science, thinned notably, and the great chief was less jubilant and talkative than of yore; so that I had almost to
drag him out of his palace on Sundays to get him to take
the air.

"I never could understand those sheets of leaves strung
about between the trees by your women and torn down
by the wind every time it blows, only to be repaired at
infinite trouble and hung up again. I notice your female
population does hardly anything but gather the leaves and
weave and reweave them."

"Oh," smiled Milto with something of his old fire, "that
is the natural occupation of women, it is what determines
a woman's quality, those who have the largest number of
leaves sewn together at any time rank highest amongst us.

Rank or quality is thus founded upon the true principle of the wind and changes with every storm. Some have pieced together fifty thousand leaves between blows; they climb into the trees with the agility of monkeys and strip them one after another, causing many to die, as you can see, which we sadly regret but cannot prevent without depriving our womenkind of the magic of life."

"Are these leaves of any use?" I questioned curiously.

"Is it not of the greatest use to perform a task which requires unspeakable labor and excels everybody else and is universally admired? Besides, our men select their wives on this principle. There is a famous rush to marry the woman who has woven the broadest sheet of leaves. If a storm comes tomorrow and reduces her to the lowest insignificance by destroying her magnificent possession, it is always remembered that at one time she had very excellent blood in her veins; contempt for her family decay is mingled with a morsel of pity, and the best of it is she at once goes diligently to work to repair her lineage by twining another patchwork of foliage. In this she is aided by the husband, who beats her if she is idle and compels her to sew while he sleeps, for it adds great luster to his person to have a wife with a wide sheet. The husbands also contrive incantations which they use with great power tho I know not with what effect against winds. When a storm is approaching they repair to the trees where they place themselves in front of their wives' handiwork on the windy side and hurl their charms at the storm, each begging it to strike his neighbors' property and spare his own."

"I have intended to study your marriage system when trade should permit, and I infer that it is closely connected with wind."

"That is its basis," said he, "and we regard the family as the foundation of society. Wind is therefore the ultimate rock of our national stability. There would be a terrible eruption of licentiousness if human passions were not restrained by the wind."

"How is that?" I exclaimed, not quite crediting the vibrations of my tympanum.

He replied: "A woman is supposed to be devoid of virtue who does not own a fabric of leaves above a certain size suspended in the trees, and whether married or not she is then exposed to general insult, from which moreover by our laws she cannot protect herself tho it be most abhorrent; but when her leafy curtain again reaches the dimensions required by virtue, her purity is restored and all men observe a courtly and even cringing reverence in their demeanor to her—so ennobling is the power of the feminine when sustained by leaves. Storms are the deadliest enemy of womankind, for by these their virtue and fortunes fall."

"What do you do if she breaks the law and repels the solicitous?"

"Put her on bread and water, gradually lessening the bread and increasing the water, in which she is obliged to stand, until she is induced to realize her dependence on the sovereign scorn of men. Sm'guth! if she will not yield then we let her die, for we do not want that kind of women in our tribe. They would be spreading their immorality."

"How does her husband take this?" asked I, feeling a shrinkage of self-complacency over my previous ignorance of the world.

"He assists in her punishment. In fact he is ashamed of her and considers himself maritally liberated until she restores her leaves to the proper standard."

"You must curse the storms and hate nature!" I groaned sympathetically. "Oh! embrace civilization, learn its better way, where those who love once love forever and expect to continue doing so when they are dead unless the proprieties of heaven are opposed to it."

Milto dashed his head violently against a stone three times, which was equivalent in that tribe to crossing himself, and his eyes eddied wildly, turning their balls so far inward that one imagined he was able to see into his own mind. "Curse the storm!" he murmured, simulating a swoon for a few seconds. "What have I done to cause you to blaspheme in my presence and tempt the wrath of God upon my stainless people? The storm is our preserver. Except for the storm our men and women would be obliged to remain together in nauseous wedlock, suffering the pangs and tortures of mutual hate after their love had died. The blessed wind comes and tears away the material structure of the leaves to which merit is hung, and society is directly liquefied again, to recrystallize anew according to the laws of true affinity and worth. We thus avoid the shocking degeneracy that would follow if we established a family on one achievement in leaves and made it lasting. The wife must continue to struggle and grow; every wind is a new stimulus to her progress, to reproduce, preserve, and increase what she has won. If this were not so and a woman, having once placed herself in the front rank of society, enriched her blood and elevated her character through the great size of her umbrageous texture, could retain her eminence and hand it down on a memory, she would soon become a worthless jade, idle, fat and proud of a bursted bubble, with a brood of lazy, detestable spawn at her ankles, having transmitted nothing but a pulpy body and soggy mind to these silly poodlets, who would shortly bring the tribe to annihilation by neighbors with more scientific marriage ideas. Do not curse the storms." He ceased speaking and toyed with one of the bosky appurtenances of the higher life.

"It is a most delicate work," I admitted, examining it with candor. "I notice that all the leaves are fitted with fine precision in the same manner to the width of a hair. This must also be designed."

"It is, for in it lies the excellency of the art. Unless the various parts of each leaf are joined to those of others in a correct style it is not regarded as a screen and the hapless artificer is still a nobody."

I went through a mental debate on the ethics of speaking further to a wild African on the chaste subject of human sex. I learned afterward that some tribes are more refined and susceptible concerning the mention of this delicate distinction than are we ourselves; that no difference between men and women is recognized in their vocabularies from an exalted native modesty transmitted from the orang, and that the young are severely rebuked and punished by their parents if they make an allusion to nature before they are thirty years old. The subject of anatomy is never allowed to enter the schools and doctors may not practise prior to their eightieth year. I was delighted at this nicety and thought these people might very well have moved in our most cultured society.

"There is some correspondence between this art of leaves and the science of licking, if my mind is clear," said I; "they both seem to be highly exact, each intricately complicated, each the supreme object of the life of a sex, and they are equally useless. Do I imagine this rightly?"

"You do," he assented rapturously. "These two objects are the very quintessence of our tribal being, after eating and killing. Our prominent lickers, those with the most eminent poles, aspire to connect themselves in marriage with the exalted ladies who possess the largest fortune in leaves, and these high women proudly disdain inferior males. So it is that our tribe's best blood ever mingles and we continually produce new generations of more cunning lickers and more artful weavers."

CHAPTER XIX

Astounding Institutions of the Horroboos

King Milto often spoke in terms of rapt affection of his bosom friend Emperor Griffelak, one of his nearest neighbors, commanding a kindred tribe one hundred miles away, with whom he had been educated in the same university. As his health grew delicate his mind became pensive and these references to his friend more frequent. A change, thought I, would do His Majesty good, for if I am not careful of him he may not last out the gold season, and the loss of the queen bee would disrupt my speculations; so I proposed that we should take an outing and pay a visit to this great section of the Horroboo nation, toward whom I also was drawn by his wonderful accounts of their advanced institutions.

"The Guardians of Food can take care of the works for a short season," I said to him, "and while the people are busy at their daily toil they will not get into mischief, tho I and you are away. Do not worry about the mines, wages are high and everyone is contented, and we have no base social agitators in our midst daring enough to flood the diggings."

Milto consented with blubbering alacrity, the color returned to his cheeks and he looked quite regal once more. So one day, mounting two dromedaries and taking on foot a large retinue of women for purposes of state, we advanced toward the mighty emperor's domain. I omit several strange incidents of the journey to plunge at once into what happened when we arrived. Milto and Griffelak carried on together like young kids. Having no equals in their own realms they could indulge in none of the ordinary and innocent pleasures of mankind unless some neighboring emperor came to spend the day at play with them

I had latterly declined all arch familiarities with Milto
since rising above his level, to keep him in his proper place.
The august potentates now relaxed; they rolled together
on the sod, raced, wrestled, shinned up trees, stood com-
petitively on their heads as a test of mental strength, and
vied with each other which could lift the larger number
of men with their teeth.   To decide their valor two powerful barricades of timber were erected, from behind which
they hurled stones at each other for several hours, thereby
honorably proving themselves equal.   A great hunt was
ordered for the afternoon of the first day.   Two hundred
youths drove in a herd of wild and dangerous hogs from
the wilderness; these they rounded up and held together
with a fierce band of African dogs of a special Horroboo
breed more ferocious than tigers and nearly the size of
horses, while the intrepid monarchs fired arrows at them
from the limbs of a tree which were regally cushioned and
backed in Amboggan plush (the Horroboo make), until
the entire battalion of savage brutes was slain.   It was
thrilling sport.   All the court ladies were present in lower
trees.

The following day was passed inspecting the institutions.
The first to which I was introduced was the Institution
of Fat Men, of which the Emperor could not speak without
an outburst of vanity quite offensive to our Caucasian
reserve.

"I noticed that you have a number of spherical people,"
said I, "but did not know they were an institution.   I should
think from appearances that you would call them the Institution of Male and Female Globular Abominations."

"So we should," Emperor Griffelak replied, "if we did
not here consider it immodest to use the term 'female';
none but me and the Medical advisors of the realm are
permitted to speak that sound."

The imperial city was peculiarly laid out.   It was a col-

lection of circles, each one being the home of a special
class of society, numbering in all sixteen. The perfection
of the social formation is there attested not only by the
great number of classes which they enjoy but by their
extreme distinctness one from the other, and by another
circumstance which made me wonder how long civilization would lag in the rear: for it is not permitted to those
of one order to pass over into the circle of any other, the
sense of distinction has been carried so high that the public roads are divided into sixteen parallel parts within which
each class is rigidly confined in its perambulations. If they
transgress they are required to submit themselves to a
painful process of purification, of no less thoroughness than
a brief boiling, afterwards they are exposed to the sun and
wind while any remaining particles of pollution or impro-
priety are removed. There was one deviation called Fat
Men's Way, a remarkable avenue reserved exclusively for
the emperor and the highest class, surrounding the royal
palace of bamboo and palm-leaves which nestled, charm-
ingly hidden among trees, in the heart of the town. Just
outside of this was the circular abode of the far-famed fat
people, which differed from the others in that it contained
the smaller circle at its center, wherein this imperial residence and its encompassing driveway were located. There
was a motive in this, tho it was not divulged till my familiarity with the institutions authorized, which was to keep
the Emperor and his conduct under the sharp espial of the
Fat. The noble monarch possessed fifty-nine other palaces
which he never used, their purpose being to sustain the
dignity of the crown.

The Fat Men's Way, or Imperial Avenue, not less than
forty feet wide and well traveled, was at the time of our
inspection crowded with an astonishing assortment of
human figures passing and repassing in either direction.
Upon platforms made of cross poles and resting on the

shoulders of natives were squatted, or reclined upon their backs sleeping, the fat ponderables who seemed to be the life of the town. These personages weighed from five to eighteen hundred pounds each; on some frames a man and woman sat together, on others a single sex alone; the smallest number of carriers was twelve, and they ranged upward to fifty who bore the weight of two vast specimens of the higher life having exactly the appearance of immense shining black sea animals and weighing together not a grain less than thirty-six hundred pounds. Their clothing was the customary fiber around the waist, but their jet black bushy hair made amends for the absence of linens, jewelry and silks. It was very thick, wiry and stiff, and twined together by natural growth to stand out an astonishing distance from the head in all directions and upward, forming a canopy impenetrable to the rays of the sun or to cloud-bursts, and useful in the recumbent posture not only as a pillow but for a mattress under the upper part of the body; while in cold weather, when in a squat posture, the owners could nearly cover themselves with this beautiful black fleece of nature. At the head of each was a woman kneading and rubbing the scalp to make the hair grow still more, while each head contained a conspicuous bunch of feathers numbering accurately just the pounds of the personage's social weight. Those who reclined, and they were the majority, were in this position from inability to sit up.

My feelings warmed toward these excellent savages, in whom philanthropy and altruism had developed in this wonderful manner, and I jotted down in my notebook what I should say to my own countrymen to shame them into more generous care of their indigent sufferers.

"This I suppose is your hospital, Griffelak," I said, touching my nose to his in approbation, their especial mark of amity; "I have never seen love carried so far as this on any part of the present planet or elsewhere, and you know I have traveled extensively. It is only on my family estates in the suburbs of Eternity that you will witness the strong sacrificing themselves for the weak. There love is sweet beyond earthly premonition; the greatest lovers are the grandest nabobs, because capacity to love is the measure of magnificence; and all are seeking new potencies of love, since no better springs of happiness have been discovered by the shrewdest investigators of delight. But here below business operations take precedence and we have no leisure to be happy in that wretchedly slow godlike way; it would be a loss of time and money, and we have to leave these beautiful raptures to callow savages and celestial angels whose time is cheap, who have neither stores nor steam, and who do not yet realize the sacred obligations of commerce. *We* have the ecstacies of mercantile phrensy, which would be quite a study for the gods and angels in their present low stage of evolution. What rare nobility for your good men—they are your clergymen I suppose—to carry your poor invalids up and down on their shoulders in the healing air. I could weep at the sight. It is truly heroic, for the wretched creatures I perceive are suffering from a contagious leprosy incident to tropical climates and the overconsumption of their friends, of which I have read, and I never saw such a sickening decomposition of human corpulence upon partially living bones before. But allow me one question: how can so many of your people afford to devote their days to this affectionate tendance, how can they secure their own livelihood while doing so? It must be a nasty drain on the labor strength of the empire, and, if I may say so courteously, a rather too exalted manifestation of love for the economic plane which your tribe has reached. Or perchance these blessed ministers are your millionaires who, having absorbed all there is, are now devoting themselves to higher things."

Griffelak glittered from head to foot with incandescent pride, and replied with that impressive grandeur which characterizes the least acts of the royal and great: "You have a wonderful insight; love is indeed the chief substance of our tribal nature; the strong delight to sacrifice themselves for the weak by permitting themselves to be carried in this condescending manner; there is truly a most expanded feeling of love within them toward those who carry them; but, Divine Sir, this is not a hospital, the bearers of these plump gentlemen and ladies are not ill nor are they rich, they are not performing this menial service for their health or to save their souls,—it is to earn a living. And as to its being a tax on the labor power of the empire for them to be so engaged, really, Esteemed Sky-dweller, it is quite the opposite, if it were not for these fat benignancies, to give the carriers occupation and nutriment, I do not see how the poor devils would live."

"How is this?" I inquired. "Do you mean that these disgusting fat monsters, who are so enormous that they can hardly stir a leg, support all this retinue of able-bodied attendants? How can they support others when they are unable to support a fraction of themselves?"

"It could only occur where the system of justice is perfect," he replied. "I have traveled among all the tribes of Africa and find none so advanced as ourselves. Listen and I will teach you the doctrine of justice quickly. But first sever your spirit from false modern logic, which is a trap we have abolished; we reason according to the eternal rules of thought-vision, which objectively creates what it mentally sees, and sees what it wants to see; we have a mind after our own hearts. These rules were anciently imparted to us by our sacred rabbit, our blessed interpreter of the mind of god to men." He settled himself and began.

CHAPTER XX

GRIFFELAK UNCOVERS THE FOUNDATIONS OF HUMAN SOCIETY

"Our food you must know consists, in addition to casual foreigners, of an earth-burrowing animal peculiar to these parts, our mainstay, in whose capture half of the tribe is regularly engaged. It is entirely owned by the fat powers which you witness. But for their generosity the tribe would starve, to say nothing of the helpless creatures who carry them up and down and who would never obtain a crust if this labor were not provided for them. The philanthropic fat stretch love to the extreme of human nature to keep their laborers alive; it is our religion; the doctrine was taught us by our greatest lawgiver, who lived seven hundred thousand years ago, knew water from land, and had stolen his information from the gods when living as their butler in a previous existence."

"It may be the very perfection of justice," said I, "and one of your fundamental economic doctrines on which probably thousands of books have been written by your college professors in a most deadly style, as I suspect from having bored through hundreds of the same kind in my country, but what is to prevent these attendants from going out to catch food for themselves?"

"That is a deep and matter and requires much learning," replied his Imperial Grandeur. "The argument may seem to you to leap here and there like a frog, but if you are educated you will be able to quickly gather up the hops and make a chain of thought. You must first know that the regular food-catchers collect as many animals as we need: food beyond that quantity is plainly valueless, for no one can use it and you do not pay for unusable things. That is self-evident, as well as being contained in our Book

of Unutterable Truth, wherein all wisdom is condensed.
Now since the Fat Super-Men own all the food, whatever
is caught must be submitted to them before anything is
done with it. If superfluous food, or more than they think
is needed, were fetched in, as it would have no value they
would give nothing to the capturers in return for its capture, and as it is their own property their duty would be
to take it from the catchers and hold it. The poor hungry
catchers having wasted their time in useless effort would
then have no food, and that is why they would be obliged
to perish of starvation if some other labor were not invented
to keep them alive. For that reason they are magnanimously engaged to carry The Fat, for which they are paid
enough food to keep their muscles from quick death. Could
a Super-God be kinder?"

"Most correctly and profoundly reasoned, Pride of the
Universe," said I, "but tell me this also: If the food brought
in is useless to everyone else and would keep the getters
of it alive, I should think it a sensible reason for letting
those who have gone to the trouble of finding it keep it."

"Outrageous!" shuddered Griffelak, "a very upheaving
doctrine! which would destroy our system of society by
knocking out the beams of speculation here and a pillar
of morals there! But we might survive seeing our society
go if it were not overthrown by charity! Can't you see
how it would debauch these carriers if the game which they
might hunt and dig, being other people's game, were given
to them for the mere labor of digging or catching it? They
must pay some useful service to the owners to preserve
their self-respect from decay. But perhaps you think it
a small thing to destroy a system of society, perhaps you
think something could take the place of carrying fat men
as a foundation of things; but you little know the depravity of man if you believe it. Carrying the fat is the
hub of our tribal chariot, our whole theory of life revolves

about it, it is the source of our food and the fountain of our happiness, for to see our beloved fat prodigies transported up and down the avenue is our grand national pastime and pride: deny us that ennobling recreation and we might as well live in the heart of a desert, or among the slovenly pigmies without an empire to crow about. Beware how you suggest the overthrow of institutions, the solid laws of nature would crash malevolently upon our heads if the fat ceased to be carried, men would refuse to believe in the reality of a personal diet, they would jeer at appetite, scout the immortality of the stomach, grow pessimistic of recuperating sleep, turn skeptical of all realities but murder, bury themselves alive in the settled faith of breathing better underground, all would be chaos again and bewildered nature would grind its elements into stardust to give the universe a new start. Beware, I say, beware."

It was my turn to experience terror before the brink I had staggered upon. "Might not something worse happen?" I whispered.

"Yes," answered this mighty Caesar in a voice that soughed and moaned through the internal horrors of my imagination, "if these carriers were permitted to go game-catching and to keep the game, they might even indulge the monstrous dream that they own the animals themselves. which would devastate the precincts of property, smash morality to elemental atoms and wash my eternal empire out of space."

All three of us now stood for a long time trembling, our knees and teeth chattering an infernal chorus. When the music died away I resumed the conversation by asking what the Fat Feeders would do with the superfluous animals if such were brought in.

"Try to eat more than they usually do," answered he, "and have the rest piled in an enclosure for decay."

"But how about those tribesmen who, you say, are regularly engaged in digging out the animals," I insisted, resolved to follow this intricate custom down to its roots; "do they not own and hold what food they collect by their own hunting?"

Griffelak bathed me in his liquid blue eyes to assure himself that I really had not mastered their economic system yet, while his delicate features were chiseled with patience. "No," he resumed, with his fascinating stately gravity; "wouldn't that be subverting the imprescriptible rights of the Fat in the very way I have shown? Whether they dig, or carry the eminent fat, is all the same; they can have only so much of the game as the Fat who own it give them, of course, and that depends exclusively on the latters' emotion. The emotion of the fat immeasurables plays an amazingly mighty role; it is the fourth foundation of the empire: myself, my throne, my fat men, and the emotion of the fat, as we call it,—that is the order of the foundations of our social edifice."

"I should like to hear why the emotion connected with fatness is so eminent a force."

"How can you ask? Is it not the first law of God that the emotion of those who own the Food controls everything? It decides the welfare of the tribe in grand and minute things, determines the quantity of food to be doled out to the populace, settles for what ends all men shall be allowed to use their strength, and so ordains our famines, plagues, diseases, birthrates, deaths, play, leisure, duration of work, wages, acts of the legislature, and in fact everything, from the adulteration of food and the poisoning of the meat supply to the value of stocks, and in a word every detail of happiness." Thus answered the knightly monarch gravely.

"Indeed," rejoined I, "it appears to be a prodigious singularity for so late an age of the world, and if my private

secretary were at hand I would give him a few sugges-
tions with which he could prepare in my name a very original essay on 'The necessity of The Fat Few for the
existence of The Lean Many,' which would probably win
me a professorship in the University of Africa, Oxford,
Berlin, or Chicago, or whatever learned cavity of the
globe I might choose to mummify in. My last secretary
wrote three brilliant books for me while I was on a little
sojourn in Venice. He was in America. I sent him the
titles and told him to go ahead, and write what he pleased,
with orders to wire me if any of his ideas were too deep
for him, and I gave him the sweet liberty to express his
own opinions life-sized, provided he did not outrun the
originality acceptable to the publishing trade. He had
been a college president who inadvertently said what he
thought on a certain lamented occasion when he was down
cellar and supposed that the house doors were locked.
When I found him he was supporting himself as a tramp,
in fact he came to my backdoor to beg permission to pull
a few weeds out of my garden for a breakfast, which at
first I steadfastly refused on account of my loyalty to the
Associated Charities, of which it turned out that he was
one of the national founders.

"My friend, said I, I am very tender hearted and I wish
to do you good, but can you tell me one righteous thing
of which indiscriminate giving is not the bane? I do not
know you, nor your wife, nor your grandmother; they
may all have been drunkards, and you may be an illegiti-
mate child for aught I know. You use good language,
but you have probably learned it in order to deceive me.
And then I read to him some of his own previously published words on the subject of charity: 'What these well-
meant philanthropies do in the way of pauperizing their
objects, in the way of undermining individual resolution
and sapping the sturdiness of individual character, must

be taken into account no less than the temporary allevia-
tions with which they are to be credited. The sum of
immediate human suffering is so great at all times, and
its evidences so apparent, that it is difficult for the tender-
hearted observer to remain philosophical in its presence,
yet we are morally bound to hesitate in coming to its relief, if by so doing we are helping to perpetuate the conditions which give it birth. That this danger is a real one
is a conclusion now so well established by sociological
investigation as to be beyond the reach of controversy.'
Now, my boy, continued I, you are a pauper albeit a very
learned one, if you speak the truth, and you were formerly
high-placed and respectable; it is possible you were the
president of the very college I graduated from, but that
is neither here nor there. You have placed yourself beyond
the reach of controversy, you purpose to upset the philosophy of my attitude for the selfish end of making me sap
the sturdiness of your individual character merely to
appease your hunger, you are attempting to undermine the
well-established conclusions of sociological investigation in
your petty personal behalf for no worthier object than a
slice of bread: Aren't you ashamed of yourself! Great
as your immediate suffering is I am morally bound to
hesitate. Sociologically I can give you nothing. It is my
Christian duty to turn you over to the police, or to give
you into the custody of Miss Dribble, National Secretary
of the Society for the Prevention of Giving Milk to the
Babies of the Poor for Fear of Degrading Their Mothers.
She will exhume your genealogy to learn whether you can
be helped without cheating the rich. This is the mission
of the Associated Charities. It is noble and kind of her
to do this, for it will use up thirty days of her valuable
life, and her salary for doing it is only two hundred dollars
a month."

"Oh, Sir," pleaded the wretch, "I was a great and pros-

perous man when I wrote those miserable words, and it
never occurred to me to investigate what hunger was
before writing a treatise about it. I was influential, proud
and rash; I wished to divert all benevolent funds from the
poor to my college; give me a crust and I will never write
on the principal subjects of my ignorance again!"

"Now is your time," I replied, "to exemplify your doctrines with resolution: what better thing can you do for the
world than to starve in behalf of the right channels of
philanthropy?"

However, after standing in the door for some time contemplating his shivering emptiness, with stern philosophical regret I began to be drawn to him and concluded to
temporarily alleviate his adversity at the risk of his refor-
mation and authority as a scientist with a little weak tea.
Cultured as he was, he was dirty from sleeping in barns.
What most prejudiced me in his favor was his wonderful
politeness, he being so polished at that time that he was
afraid to speak above a whisper lest he should offend somebody. I had to place an ear trumpet near his mouth to
get the slightest idea what he was attempting to say.

"I took him into my house and had him washed and
subjected to a course of feeding, meanwhile having one
of my servants pump up his lungs, alternately inflating
and exhausting them with a bellows, to strengthen them
for audible conversation. When he had in some measure
recovered the use of his languages, of which he had nine,
and recalled to his features the vanished shadows of a
few forgotten smiles, I led him to a structure that adorns
my place for the free expression of opinion. Its walls
are several feet thick, padded with formidable layers of
embalmed literary eloquence warranted to kill both sound
and the germs of thought, containing neither window nor
door, and the entrance is through a winding passage under
ground starting downward from the bottom of my cellar,

where a brace of famished bulldogs guard the opening to discountenance the curiosity of strangers. Having hoisted the doctor up through the floor of this fortress and bidden him to speak his mind bravely to the void I departed. In the ceiling, by a deft contrivance of my architect—who by the way is so much below me in social standing that I never speak to him on the street and frequently cuff him when we are debating architectural plans alone—is an even-tempered machine for recording one's words and serving them up unfeelingly on another occasion. You know not these tell-tale incorruptible contrivances here, Griffelak, and I am sorry. You could have your wife's words re-engraven on your heart whenever they faded, without calling her back.

"However, into this vocabulary-vessel the good president unconsciously talked himself, being so delighted with the sensation of courage that I could hardly draw him out of the fort to his meals. I kept him in there eighteen hours a day and resolutely forbade him the use of this hall of heroism another minute in the twenty-four. A copyist transcribed what he said out of the embalmer and I found him to be a very polychromatical genius. He had many honest ideas of his own, which he now permitted to escape for the first time, and which led me to suspect that other great professors might develop some rudimentary independent thoughts if I could only get them into my trap. To cut a long story short, for I know Your Exaltation is wasting away to talk yourself, I published all he said under the very seductive title, 'The Literary Explosions of a Tramp,' which the public devoured with insatiable horror and avidity. I was afraid to sign my name to it for fear of violence from the government, and its authorship was attributed to an organization of assassins, tho from internal evidence the learned world proved it to be a buried copy of the writings of one of those Chicago monsters so entertainingly hanged a few years ago for saying what everybody is saying now, and by preaching which a recent president rose to fame. Little mattered it to me, for I made more out of it than Walter Scott earned in all his lifetime of dingy industry. When the storm subsided a little I acknowledged the authorship, explaining in the preface that I was its sole, true and unaided originator. I felt no pangs for stealing my secretary's work, for all writers of great books do this now. True geniuses, poor dogs, must be contented to sell their brains and suppress their names. I don't say the Money Sack created all mind, but it owns all.

"My reputation was thus established as a transcendent writer, which, on the strength of that brilliant book, it has remained ever since. I am now able to emit the greatest twaddle in book form on any subject or science I deign to treat of, all that is necessary to revolutionize human thought in that department being its emanation from my supposed pen. I particularly enjoy these convulsions of thought and sometimes launch several of them in the same department of learning at the same time on conflicting sides, to watch the sputter created. A great writer can be burdened with no principles. To have human beings behave like a body of minstrels each playing a different measure, or like several unfriendly vortical motions in the same atom, or like a group of dissonant souls combined into one personality, in a word to have all men idiots, dervishes or devils, gives the author artistic tingles and something to write about. So, being a great man, produced by high heaven to amuse the world, it would be a pitiful weakness for him to possess principles and to use them to shape mankind into something better than idiots and devils.

"Sometimes I allow my gardener to write the treatises and sometimes my coachman; my butler does it best, however, for he is blessed with a most horrible indigestion from overeating and emits the most startling hypotheses.

My name carries the authority that sells the book. But I have wandered from my university president. Well, finding him a man of parts I presented him with a box of blacking, loaned him a brush, and engaged him as my amanuensis. He is now writing books for me at a salary of ten dollars a week and boarding himself while I travel. What were you saying when I interrupted? Oh, yes, that the fat people's emotion governs everything with you, and I thought that principle of government a little archaic if not tangled. But go on as if I had not interposed a word."

CHAPTER XXI

The Terrible Potentate Teaches Me Political Economy

"It is very simple," resumed the Emperor, who had listened with charming attention to my remarks, "and especially does credit to the wisdom of our thoroughbred cherubs—the fat. They have divided their emotions into nine grades and thus with astonishing niceness determine the welfare of a people: they are a food barometer divided into nine parts. 'Nine' is the exceeding extremity of generous feeling at which, besides allowing the people as much food as they need to eat, they confer upon them their cast-off garments and a lock of their hair. The emotion of the fat at this high pressure is nearly fatal to life, and for the preservation of these our noble lamps of beauty and intellect it is not expected to be felt over once in ten years. When their emotion sinks to 'one' food disappears and we have a terrible famine from heaven, there is wailing and gnashing of unoccupied teeth, children die like grasshoppers, the wrath of God is upon us, which continues until the gluttons' emotion begins to return. They hover between two and four when they are what we call normal, which is all the emotion our corpulencies can regularly stand without harm."

"I suppose," I said, "that this is a manner of saying, with exalted respectfulness for the fat gentlemen and their pudgy consorts, as if their omnipotence caused the calamity, that at certain periods the game runs scarce and all the population fare without."

"Not at all," cried the Emperor merrily, "the quantity of game has nothing to do with it, nor are we silly enough in this cultured zone to invent soggy fictions to solace empty stomachs. The food never runs slack, but from time to time the globy censors seem to think that the people are indulging in it too freely and shut off the supply, which they can properly do because it is all theirs. I have known thousands to die on such occasions and to breed our principal plagues. The gluttons go on with their eating as usual and the game hunters continue gathering the game tho swallowing none of it; what the amiable fat cannot eat is by their order deposited in their enclosures to decay."

"By Hercules and Heaven!" I exclaimed in petrifaction, "what is this I hear! I have never paid a visit to the sub-cutaneous regions of existence where, I am told, this is one of the sardonic novelties, without baptism and allegiance to which I understand a man there is no good devil, but this I. declare is the first time I knew it to be practised anywhere above ground. Tell me then, and do not beguile yourself with my credulity as a bud in these parts, do your food-finders go on collecting game and even while they are in a dying condition from hunger for that very food, deposit it in the private wicker yards of the surfeited fat to spoil, because these bloated mammoths are opposed to their eating it? Do you assert this?"

"You have hit the nail," grinned Griffelak.

"Then I say here in public, taking my life in my hand,

fat or lean, cannibalism or gallows, it is the most refined act of savagery ever perpetrated without the assistance of newspapers," which I declared at near the top of my voice, boiling wroth.

"Certainly it is," agreed His Highness; and would you believe it? he seemed to fancy I had delivered myself of a happy compliment to his country! "Certainly it is; we are modestly proud of our refinement and the surpassing advancement of our savagery. It is necessary for us to keep our business standards steeple-high, if you understand me, for we are much looked up to by the vulgar races on all sides; all the tribes within a thousand miles, spellbound by the grandeur of our free liberties, are hastening to build up a fat stock to liberally oppress them as we are oppressed."

Inasmuch as he was serious I gave my indignation a douche of caution and clothed my moral ardor in the stately equilibrium of the passionless scholar. Said I: "Feelings are like birds of the air flying hither and thitherward, emotion is but a chance wave of the psychic sea, an accidental ripple in the foam of consciousness: do your brawny intellectual folk accept these fleeting perturbations of a few tons of half-living fat as the reverend cause of all their weal and ill? Isn't this thunderingly casual and arbitrary, if I may take a stormy illustration from chance and nature?"

"If you think so," Griffelak replied; "you have studied the marvels of soul and ghostly truth with a smoky telescope. Do you venture to call the united emotion of these loftiest mountains of our stock, our largest thinkers, our mightiest feelers, our weightiest citizens, our first society men and women, our smart set, who look more like gods than men and have as many cubic feet of emotion in them as cattle, dare you call their emotion casual, arbitrary, bilious? Sir, a wink from one of these globules of glory gives you a vested interest in the stars and a farm on the surface of eternity; after that honor you walk on stilts lest your feet should touch the ground and again vulgarize you. Divine oil! heavenly adipose! your emotion is from Above. If you are lodged in a man's skin and can feel, you represent an ordinance of nature, the will of the one God. Is anything accidental in the universe? Have not all things their fathomless cause in the abysmal caverns of holy reality? Is not man's feeling a sacred signal from the supreme essence? a wireless message from the vibrant braincells of the All? It mirrors the placid eddies of the purling mind of the Almighty, duplicates his sensations, re-edits his sentiments, indexes his purpose, communicates his will. We have appointed our noblest brethren to feel for us all, they act but as conductors and depositories of God's emotions, when they feel that we are eating too much we know that it is God's feeling, when they feel that a plague is needed to unflesh and depopulate us we recognize it as a deep-planned dispensation of Heaven; we go to consult their emotions as we interrogate entrails concerning destiny, the sky concerning storms, the rain concerning water, and we bow meekly to their holy blows with hearts bursting with thanks that God's ways to us are not ambiguous."

"If you would call these emotions economic laws I should consider you extremely wise," said I, "and should see oceans of fish-sense in what you say, but so long as you fail to name them properly the thing seems to me rather a frog pond of idiocy. Economic laws are direct from God, but where you wilfully insert a ganglion of human emotions between, one cannot avoid the horrible suspicion that there is some devil in the last delivery. Stick close to economic laws, my friend, which are the most fashionable

_____

*It is unnecessary to inform the civilized that Adam Smith was God's latest instructor of any note. He coached the Almighty through difficulties for a century.

babblings of God since Adam Smith*; then you will be as appropriately miserable as the most tortured creatures with power to feel can be."

"Suffering!" bawled Griffelak. "Verily indeed! We suffer for our discipline, that is why it is sent: it is the untarnishable glory of our nation to have found this out and made ourselves good and sublime by subjugating ourselves to all the sorrow we can collect. We know from the cruel anguish we feel that it is sweet for us to become emaciated and die when our fat demigods are moved from on high to restrict our food. This was also certified by our great lawmakers in mephitic antiquity."

"When these famines come do the fat ones also deny food to Your Majesty?"

"Of course not, for I am supreme and perfect without starvation. Starving can only improve the poor."

"Being passionately in love with the beauty of anguish for the Kingdom of the Fat Men's Emotions' sake, I think your good people prefer stripes and torments and shackles and tribulations and racks to a square meal in paradise, if The Fat ordain them, and would joyously refuse to eat terrapin in their last hours of hunger, if some one stuffed it into their mouths against the orders of the Obese."

"You are right," said the Emperor; "the popular reverence for religion and the Law of Emotion would prevent them from eating in that case. Your Economic Laws we know nothing about, but we sometimes call our Gluttons the 'Laws of Divine Emotion,' to indicate the serious, necessary and eternal character of their feelings. They who starve are so thoroughly in accord with the starvation system of things that they would uphold the decrees of the gluttons against themselves in the face of armies and navies, and would go to their death fighting for the right of the Fat to starve them. That is another sure proof that the gluttons' consciousness is founded on the Eternal."

"It is an excellent thing to call this emotional principle laws of some kind," said I. "Laws have a permanent sound. To be sure it is always the emotion of the owners of property that decides everything and lies behind all laws, but for heaven's sake don't let it be known; it would upset civilization if not savagery."

"I tell you we are perfectly satisfied with the truth," he repeated. "Is the civilized man so stupidly cowardly that, not daring to face the evil oppressors that grind him, he names their tyranny with silly phrases like 'nature's laws' to hide the shame of his craven spirit? We are above such weakness. Emotion it is, and our people worship it naked and known; we have no need to clothe it with lies, tho civilization—do you call it?—may. We are proud of being oppressed. We live for it."

CHAPTER XXII

THE ORIGIN OF HORROBOO GRANDEUR

I gave up instructing him with resignation, and presently asked how these towers of surplus humanity came to be the owners of all the wild animals in existence on which the tribe lived. Did they invent the animals, or create them, or cultivate them, or inherit them from Adam, or what?

"Nothing of the sort," His Highness answered amused; "these fertile creatures pour down into our plains from the inaccessible mountain folds where they breed, burrowing their way; freely they descend from heaven in the most generous sense, and we are accountable to the heavenly powers for a right use of them. Their ownership was acquired by the fat men twelve thousand years ago in the reign of my first ancestor. It was indeed this

episode that made him Emperor, and he left a chronicle
of his life which tells the deathless history. When he was
born the tribe was wallowing in the slimy dank of degradation; they had no king and no fat; the people were monotonously happy, all of them occupying the dismal sing-song
level of perfect bliss; they were all kings, for none in-
fringed upon another and all were highest; disease was
unknown and food abounded; there was no word in the
language for famine, nor had they the name death, for
all departed so contentedly and beautifully at the age of a
hundred and ten that none who remained were sorrowful
or mourned. This ludicrous dearth of sorrow lasted until
my far-smiting ancestor was ninety years old, the comfort
and happiness of all being so radiantly complete that he
felt himself continually impelled to suicide. It was unen-
durable! There was no satisfaction in having everybody
equal! In our annals we call this lugubrious time the
Beast Age because all were contented. Peace and good
will reigned, there was no ambition to gnaw and defile,
pride and contempt there could not be for these vices
flourish not among the equal."

"Great Griffelak," cried I with antecedent compassion,
"how did it happen that the Horroboo nation survived that
execrable period? The deadliest terror of Christian mankind today is its dream of Utopia, they scare evil children
into goodness with its black horrors, and picture it in the
jails to torture the criminal, the poor foam with frenzy
against its saving hopes, but to have had the real thing
right in your country, living with it from day to day in
ideal loveliness and delight, must have been a combination
of hellfire, delirium tremens and hydrophobia. Go on, I
hold my breath to hear of your miraculous deliverance."

"Then," said Griffelak, "occurred the change that brought
to pass our magnificent evolution to savagery. One day
the tribe was sitting in the afternoon sun, a careless glad-

some multitude of laughing ebullient children, without a woe in their hearts or a peril in their firmament. A flock of wild geese flew far overhead, and one through accident or age stumbled in its course and descended to the earth in the very midst of our joyous people. The nearest rushed playfully forward and plucked out its feathers, so that shortly the poor bird was utterly bare, while its despoilers decorated their bodies with its former apparel. Only about a hundred person had secured a share of these feathers, and the remainder, when they saw their lucky companions strutting about in the bedraggled ornaments, were direfully chagrined and demanded the privilege of wearing them part of the time. But the hundred would not hear of this, because, said they, 'the goose having fallen near us, heaven evidently intended us to have all its feathers.' But they agreed to allow the others to enjoy a feather for one hour in return for an earth-bird.* This was considered highly just, and was willingly consented to; the lucky feather-owners were able to relinquish hunting, they received such an overplus of food that they were abidingly sick, which was recognized as a testimony of divine interest, and the singular phenomenon of fatness made its appearance.

"Still, tho eating all the while and scarcely taking time to sleep, so great was their fidelity to the rights of their stomachs, they could consume but a fraction of the flesh that their feathers earned for them; wherefore it came into their heads to build enclosures for the reception of the surplusage, imagining that their stomachs would grow if constantly exercised and reach the capacity of digesting all their savings. It is a fact that their stomachs did enlarge, and with very notable consequences as the ages passed, but not so fast as their food went to decay. Seeing this and mourning greatly at the loss of it to themselves, they

---

*They sometimes called the tribal article of food by this name because if it chanced to escape from its burrow it would fly.

arranged with the hunters to open an account and have the animals due delivered in the future. By and by, of course a while after my first noted ancestor's time, they figured up the debt and found that more animals were owed than the world could ever produce, so that it burst upon them that they owned the total stock of animals and all their latent progeny forever. Thereupon they naturally rescinded the feather wearing compact and no longer permitted the hunters to wear feathers at all, since they had nothing to pay in return. It was a gigantic relief to the people to be delivered from the burden of owning the animals; few beings are equal to the mill-stone worries of possession; the population now shifted all these tearful responsibilities on to the measureless ribs of the fat, and went forward with light hearts and lighter stomachs, gathering food just as they had done before, without the crushing affliction of owning the shortest hair of it, or the carking abrasion of calculating whether to eat it or not. These topmost theorems of mighty mathematics the fat men solved for them.

"Afterwards geese became very plentiful; the people, sorry for what they had done, threatened unrest; prompt action was immediately taken however by the Stomachs— an honorary title of the Fat,—who instantly appropriated all the wild geese in the sky on the principle of having owned the first goose, thereby preserving the country from the frightful throes and death pangs of revolution. It was then that the Counsellor Class arose, but you must be tired; let us now dine on a few boiled babies that I see coming, the children of those who can get nothing to do in our celebrated sun-shaming commonwealth, and after you have slept I will introduce you to more enlightened astonishments."

CHAPTER XXIII

Horroboo Spinsters

The babies were a little lean, since the parents had had nothing to feed them, but appeared to have been slaughtered in time to preserve their youthful flavor. I sampled them all, but one I could not eat, which from being killed too soon had the flavor of bob-veal.

"It is not uncommon," remarked Griffelak, crunching a collar-bone, "for women whose husbands are out of employment to destroy themselves in order to furnish these husbands with food to preserve their lives. The wives esteem this a peculiar ceremony of love because they then become deeply involved in the essence of their lords and remain so according to our scientists several years, which ensures the duration of love for that length of time, for in loving himself a man then cannot help loving his wife. It is the form of death most desired by our choicest women, partly owing to the well-known devotion of that sex to those who do not love them and partly because it assures them of immortality for seven years. There is now considerable lack of employment, which seems to be growing, for there are heavenly omens that the fat providences are contracting their bowels of emotion; there would be much suffering if it were not for this special and chosen class of women to fall back on in such crises. They are called child-women, for that they never marry until late in life, and seldom bear children, whence they retain most of the attributes of children down to old age, sometimes never parting with them. They are also our best women, and there is a shrewd motive and purpose in this, for being our brightest female intellects there is danger that they may fall into the loose and libidinous custom of using their minds, and even sink to the profligacy of imparting their

thoughts to their offspring, leading to the execution of some
great design, perhaps to the super-damnable crime of annihilating the omnipotence of the fat. Hence our sagacious
fat sunbeams take pious measures that these mentally las-
civious women shall have no children, or, if any, so far on
in life that they lack the lustiness of iconoclasm. Chastity
with us consists in avoiding the conception of thoughts;
intercourse of young minds is therefore considered most
threatening since it might lead to a pregnancy of ideas,
and is prohibited by statute; the most chaste women are
those who, being most fitted to think, punctiliously avoid
doing so; feminine virtue is keeping the mind a *tabula rasa,*
or a piece of white paper untarnished by mental activities;
if a man approaches a woman with the well-known evidences of dishonorable design to lead her astray into
thought, she will remain a psychical virgin all her days
before she will gratify him. Bodily and spiritual chastity
thus go together.

"These women, having been purified of their psycho-
physical infirmities by abstinence from everything, and de-
ploring only that there is not something else sunny and
pleasurable to abstain from, are crowned with a chaplet
of dead leaves to be worn in public as a testimony of their
immaculateness, for notification to mankind that their virtue is absolute; and the reverence thenceforward paid them
by men is of a most touching character, for they revere
them so highly that as the women approach the men all
go over to the other side of the street that they may not
contaminate these angel essences by a closer presence. It
is the will of the fat that this shall be so. While such
women are still young and beautiful the men are afraid
of them for fear they may lose the esteem and favor of
the fat, and do not ask them in marriage, for nothing could
more endanger our fat system than intelligent children.
When the fat withdraw their good will from anyone the

omens portend a private famine for him. We call it a private famine when a man is dislodged from employment by the fat lords, and a public one when they cut off the whole nation's food. Owing to these overhanging dangers the men themselves are not a little wary of anything in woman that savors of intellect, and know that the symptoms will pass away if her passion of love is put upon a permanent diet of disinfected wind. Socially enforced spinsterhood is therefore used as a cure and is applied to those females who exhibit the most alarming signs of intelligence.

"The men also have a little fear on their own account, being haunted with the nightmare that women might make some things better if they should acquire sufficiently expanded minds to realize the stupidity of the men, which illumination the males oppose with dreadful vehemence. Having now by dint of prayer, commercial thievery and politics brought the earth down to its vilest inventible plight, the men maintain a determined inquisition against all that would reveal their lazy and degraded natures to women. They carefully teach women that things have to be as they are, altho the brutish men themselves knowingly made things what they are, and keep them so. Tho from this perpetual attitude of mind the men have nearly all grown to look like sneaking servile donkeys (when they are allowed food enough to look like anything but sneaking ghosts), strangely enough the women think them very beautiful and can be got to marry the disgusting slim cravens any time.

"We have a party which we call The Changeless, who carry out their principles against improvement with adorable devotion and subtle logical force. They consider every change immoral, since it might chance to improve something. A wicked change, according to this High Stationary Set, and one which reveals the iniquity of the soul of nature, is the advancement of beauty in children as they mature, but this it is proposed to rectify by cutting atrocious furrows in their faces, paring off the end of a beautiful nose or breaking it, and taking other moral precautions against perfection. This is a miraculous prophylactic against progress in the countenance and establishes a unity between the features of man and those of society by making them equally stationary and ugly. We recognize that if it is dangerous for men to depart from present ways and change into something better now, it was a mistake for mankind to have left older ruts and advanced to present standards in the past, so that progress was always sinful."

Griffelak paused out of breath for he had spoken rapidly with an impetuous relish for his subject. I nudged his memory on a momentous point. "Why would there be suffering in times of depression but for these excellent child-women, or prolonged virgins?"

He answered: "They are a reserve fund for the men who lose their work. Such men being utterly destitute and having not a morsel in their larders, marry a child-woman from stark desperation. In gratitude the women take their own lives to become their husbands' cold lamb, preserving them until the fat men's prejudice against their eating wears off and they are reprieved from idleness. After their long maidenhood there is nothing earthly in the love of these chastened ex-children; one who marries them enters into the thin ethereal emotions of heaven, which has been called by one of our poets 'the spaceless infinite of ineffable intangibility'; in this vacuum of holiness the men would die speedily if they did not eat their sainted wives with dispatch. But the women, having immaculated themselves by mortal abstinence through all their lovely prime and parted with their carnal womanly potencies to feel, hasten to immolate themselves in the invisible, and die chanting an immortal dirge named 'Spectral Pinions

of Phantom Purity'; death is the apotheosis of their un-
sullied perfection, for they make excellent phantom beef-
steaks tho good for nothing else but virtue."

CHAPTER XXIV

GRIFFELAK THE GREAT

The last cutlet being devoured we turned our conversa-
tion back into heroic fields, and I inquired of His August
Solemnity how his family came into the purple. "Griffelak
First," said I, "must have combined the eminences of
Achilles, Ulysses, Dick Turpin, George Washington, Beel-
zebub, Elijah, Judas and President Kruger."

'Well," answered His Majesty, "convey your mind back
to the episode of the goose. Griffelak the Great, altho
he was not then great, was, I have remarked, ninety years
old and in the apple of his prime. He was the mightiest
youngster of them all, except in his headpiece as I shall
prove to his credit by and by. Time passed and the people
began to send hungry glances back to the days when they
were equal, contented, happy and perfectly fed. Some
mourned and were not comforted for the loss of all these
things by the glory of wearing a goose-quill. The death-
rate rose like the tide, they were tossed about on the surges
of turgid anxiety to collect the needless food rent for their
feathers, and a mortal misery submerged the race. From
the beginning there had been a remnant not exceeding a
fiftieth of the tribe who did not appreciate the value of
goose feathers and cared not to wear them, preferring diet.
They stubbornly rejected the contract in which the others
had engulfed themselves, and furnished no surplus victual
to the fat; they prognosticated that the people's food-debt
to the Gorgers would soon out-volume the sands of the

sea, and they resolved to hold their claim to the food stock unmortgaged; nor would they be silent regarding the scandalous wrong, but were ceaselessly assailing its perpetrators and proclaiming the future sorrows of the people. By this unseemly interference with natural law they incensed the fat, who subtly stirred up the feather-lovers against them as seditious traitors. Their lives were never safe, and finally the feather-owners, well knowing that a truth-teller is a brand of fire in a rotten world, seized an occasion when the people were a perfect furnace of wrath against the patriots who had implored them to resume their rights to bread and butter, incited the masses to put themselves in chains for revenge, and while these raging masses were surfeiting their madness upon their own shackled bodies and on their posterity, caused them to vote the strongest man in the tribe to be their emperor, to protect them against their hated saviors. Martial law however was not rescinded until they had discovered the strongest man. His residence was in the mountains and he never visited the borough except on market days, when he was liable to swoop down with a club as large to their terrified eyes as a tree and to carry off several of his fellow countrymen for his private refection. He was distinguished from common men also by the length of his bodily hair which sprouted out several inches in soft consistency on every part of his being. His ancestry was remarkable and richly suited to kingship, for he was descended from a long line of complete idiots on both sides, none of whom could express their range of ideas with more than three slightly varying grunts.

"They transmitted their idiocy unimpaired from generation to generation by a system of marriage something more than divine, for they considered the family so sacred that it should never be allowed to alter or perish but be endowed with an enduring impregnable stability unknown in the lecherous universe, by shutting it solidly within itself. They were of course monogamists; as for divorce they hewed any brother into first principles whose grunt contained a lush suggestion of it, and their famous family validity was cemented by the blessed sacrament of parents regularly marrying their children and prohibiting all wanton intercommunication with stranger blood. The family once formed was immediately sealed up and remained with its contents perfect, absolute, and the same forever. There could be no doubt of either the stability or holiness of their marriage institution under these indissoluble circumstances. Besides accomplishing the preservation of idiocy and guarding the chemical chastity of their veins, they banished all happiness and intelligence from the marriage relation, making its sanctity heavenly. Altho their minds decayed under this vertical nuptial regimen, as was shown by the disappearence of two of their grunts, their bodies throve prodigiously and Griffelak the destined Great was endowed with a muscular force equal to that of an army of meanly-begotten Horroboos on a lower level of matrimony. Hence he was in all points the proper king for the occasion, and Mr. Carlyle, had he been living, could have written some glowing volumes of odd panegyric of him, for which his skin, owing to its vastness, had it been taken off and dried, would have formed the inspiring parchment.

"The first problem was to catch this able monarchist, a delicate business since his animosity to his foully begotten congeners was so clean and pious that he slew them on sight. By means of a great trap set between two mountains he was finally captured however, the whole tribe uniting in the drive and afterward bearing him down to the plain in their clasped arms. There the hair was shaved off him up to the neck by several barbers with sharp stones, to give him a kind of undress coating of civilization before he entered into the solemn contaminations of authority.

"He was the ideal choice of the feather-men. They shrewdly humored his family prejudices, granting that his blood had trickled down in a straight sluice from the empyrean apex, that divorces and love marriages were the only simon-pure crimes in Africa, and that the possession of intelligence indicated great lack of intellect, after which they could do whatever their whims invited with him. Apart from his marital megrims he was as docile as a chambered carp. They entertained themselves pulling his tail, of which there was still some left, and jerking the returning hairs out of his body, with great pain to him but more delight, for they would say to him that it was done to see his blue blood flow after the hair, the very sight of such blood throwing him into convulsions of pride. If His Idiot Majesty sometimes grew angry when the feathery fat patricians tweaked his nose in savage sport, it needed but a declaration that in theory they agreed with him in everything, and the alarming monster immediately melted again into an amiable mess of soft-soap, sap and honey. They used him to wash their soiled linen and feet, and for other herculean tasks; he chastised their enemies and carried their friends on his back, trotting up and down with his load in front of their fatnesses' palaces for hours; he cleaned their chimneys and blacked their shoes, he stood guard at their gates all night while they slept and carried away the hillocks of greasy bones which remained after their meals in the daytime; in a word he was a pattern emperor, tenderly obedient to his amorphous masters, the Money-Bags, and about all he asked in return was the imperial privilege to strut upon his legs, yell, now and then kill somebody, and brandish his prejudices and his ancestors.

"Such an one was my peerless progenitor, Griffelak First and The Great. The fat soon called on him to slaughter a few traitors to them, which earned him the right to wear

three fish-bones in a raised triangle on the hair of his chest
in witness that he was the savior of his country. George
Washington Griffelak, he is sometimes styled by his modern admirers, but some secretly name him Judas Caesar
Griffelak. Of those priceless fish-bones there are only a
few in our inland country, lifting their value above the
avarice of purchase. The executed traitors were those
truculent clodpolls who had refused to sign over their property in the food to the fat, those arrant opponents of commercial growth for whom pits and millstones were too kind.
Let me add proudly that this crowned heavy-weight was
the first to use force in the tribe and that he inaugurated
the constitutional custom of putting progressive malefac-
tors to death. I may here run ahead of my story to say
that a later Griffelak purged the commonwealth of all the
descendants of these cankerous recalcitrants. It was when
the fat calculators found by Horroboo logarithms that the
renters of their feathers owed them more food than all
known breeds of eaten animals could ever procreate, and
foreclosed their mortgage on all future flesh. Those who
had never rented feathers declared themselves exempt from
this act and insisted on their right to the animals as before.
Here the Counsellors saved commerce by citing an ancient
statute, lost and obliterated from record and that never
existed, which restricted the claim of these unruly men to
the animal offspring over and above those which all the
existing animals and their descendants could reproduce.
Since this vanished statute was said to have been enacted
some centuries after the goose fell to earth, with the provision that it should act backward, the proof was clinch-
ing, and the tribe, being much addicted to dancing, drunkenness and philosophy, was whirled away into delirious
conviction by the argument. The Counsellors further convicted the protesters of being evil, by using the well-known
annihilating theological argument that 'evil is evil,' so

leaving the obstructors with no theoretic ground to stand on.

"Nevertheless my active forefather was more useful than the thinkers: he choked the objectors to death one by one wherever he met them, and having restored harmony by exterminating all dissonance, confirmed the title of the Fat to all the food forever."

CHAPTER XXV

The Chief Eaters and Their Advanced Anatomy

"Were the feather-owners very happy in their new vocation while these adventures were in the wind?" I asked.

"Neither then nor for ten thousand years afterward," admitted he. "According to the record this period was consumed in adapting themselves to the privileges of their gastric regimen. How they missed the pleasure of hunting! for they could no longer go out into the fields to mingle frolicsomely with their former equals, now illimitably beneath them; all their manly exertions and felicities ceased, leaving a bad appetite, eternal colic, appendicitis, and grandeur as their only respites from mortal tedium; they sat at home in a noble dining palace hollowed out in the earth, and ate and slept day and night in the same spot, and hated and frequently assassinated each other to enliven the maddening monotony — when they could get enough awake to do so. They died young, scarcely ever exceeding thirty years, having thus reduced their earthly residence below one-third of its normal period; but they said a merry life is the thing, and we have secured the illustrious and abiding boon of greatness; and the merry fellows rotted through their brief youthful years with loathsome diseases for which there were no names because they had never

been seen or heard of before. At first they strove to prick
their spirits up by a daily mimic hunt in the aristrocratic
seclusion of the palace yard, a hole in the ground two hundred feet square, where they waddled after kittens with
a furious simulation of excitement, but they missed the
jocund presence of their former equals, now reduced inferiors, while their growing corpulency and distempers
greatly restricted their power to waddle. The vulgar
appearance of usefulness was delicately extracted from
these hunts by their austere avoidance of catching anything,
which would have savored of a relation to the lower and
productive classes, whereas the motions of hunting were
compatible with their exalted station, if tarnished with no
practical results. Weakness from overfeeding and chronic
blood poisoning soon caused them to detest and abandon
even these formal motions.

"They ate and slept in perpetual fear of murderers,
owing to the sudden prevalence of insanity, which had
burst out in the tribe nobody for the life of him could
tell why, altho the prophets had sat with the tops of their
heads against one another for twenty-seven nights investi-
gating themselves for the cause. At the end of that time
one of them, in the lowest tones and most modest manner,
had inquired of the head of his neighbor if the madness
might not arise from popular despondency over withdrawal
of the food supply, causing general famine, for which
blaspheming of the fat the others had promptly kicked him
to death. Another vociferously roared that it sprang from
base popular jealousy toward the good fat men in their
honest possession of the feathers and bread, a murky pro-
letarian sentiment deservedly punished with insanity from
heaven,—and this blameless seer was presented by his
comrades with a tripod of beans, and by the fat was adorned
with a new rank called 'Fat Bags' Advocate,' in recognition of his reptilian insight.

"We have a surgery which alone preserved the line of the fat through ten thousand years of stress and pain. An aperture was made in the wall of the stomach through which the superflux food could be automatically ejected as they ate; in this manner they could eat without cessation and yet without bursting; digestion and fattening advanced steadily, while the admirable safety-valve preserved the anatomical system from destruction. The aperture, if I know myself, was like a foreign market out of which the fat capitalists who, God bless them, were bound to eat everything so that the people might get nothing, could naturally discharge the national surplus from their system and still eat and still not explode, but you are better versed in that topic."

I assured Griffelak of the brilliancy of his suspicions, and he went on.

"Toward morning nightly, when the stomachs made their nearest approach to emptiness, servants came and introduced into the holes the nozzles of bellows which they worked to blow the stomachs full of air, distending them as far as they would go and thus gradually increasing their executive capacity. Consequently a notable change has taken place in the fat men's internal departments and they are not like other men's. To accommodate the preternatural quantity of work required of it the stomach entered into competition with the other vital organs, usurping their space and diminishing their size, whereby the blood assumed a peculiar superior nature, having retained a great many of the excellent qualities which the kidneys and other thievish organs are wont to pilfer and carry out of the food to the body's loss. It is therefore no dream that the fat are composed of different blood and a higher nature than the rabble population, that their essence is endowed with rich attributes wasted and rejected from the common anatomy, that their spirits contain various acids

and salts severely indispensable to perfection, that they are
a new creation higher than man but not quite so high as
God, that their blood is an ichorish white liquid middling
between melted grease and glue. Naturally these superior
creatures with their refined and attenuated emotions consider redblooded men a gross species of tamed animals or
domesticated gibbon, with which their spirits have nothing
in common."

"Have you an inner map of this rare anatomy?" I cried
ardently; "I should like to carry a portrait of these expansion stomachs and abdomens back to the United States, to
patent and suggestively sell to the rich."

"I can give you a pretty accurate description," replied
the Emperor, "and you can make the drawings. The central stomach found it hugely laborious to digest for its
distant dependencies—the legs and arms and head, and
therefore organized a branch stomach in each of these
provinces. The one in the brain is peculiarly interesting,
occupying a noble arena in the central region of the enceph-
alon, where it furnishes the substance of thoughts direct
to the brain-cells, without the delay of heart-beats and
arterial journeys. These thoughts are many grades nearer
the true nature of things than common men's thoughts,
since they come straight out of the food in its natural state
in the head, free from the numerous transformations of
its being and removals from spirit wrought in lower men
by its confused wanderings through the body in digestion.
They thus assimilate ultimate being and reality unchanged
out of the food into their thoughts.* We have therefore

---

*We have been very snobbishly censured by some foreigners for our
cannibalism, remarked Griffelak aside soon after, but here we have its
scientific basis; and he asserted that it was no counsel of perfection
that the loitering peoples of Europe and America would some day arrive
at its adoption. Since cooking, he said, destroys the life of grain and
meat, the cooking nations feed on ashes; we prefer to feed life with life, rather
than with death. But it is of no less moment what forms of living cells
we feed on, whether high or low: now grains and vegetables are low

the highest system of philosophy ever introduced into the world, but of course it is only comprehensible to the fatmen, a mind not fed like theirs by the metaphysical essence of food being unable to grapple with the mechanism of their conceptions. We know for example the exact nature of God, where he is and how large; we have a correct analysis of his fairly numerous essences; nothing remains to be learned about Being, Spirit, Consciousness, Thought, Matter, Energy, or Life, all having been comprehended in their most ultimate meaning; matter has been transmuted into consciousness and consciousness into matter. The chemical composition of Sin and Love has been untangled, all through the operation of the mind-stomach, which conveys all these things in their natural state directly into thought, thereby unveiling their most secret properties and essence. Love of any quality and intensity can now be manufactured in the laboratory, and being swallowed or inhaled will invade the system of the swallower with its nature. A particular kind of love has to be compounded with reference to each individual toward whom the emotion is to be felt, for no two loves in the universe are alike. Sin turned out to be an indigestion of ideas—which will be obviated hereafter by the mental stomach. In truth everything marvelous has been reduced to the simplicity of light by our great fat thinkers, so that the humblest

---

and fit only to make brutes, as they do; the animals are one stage higher, yet if eaten can only produce inferior beastlike forms of men, and very bloodthirsty ones as civilization shows; but when men are eaten, and especially if devoured alive, the system of the devourer is nourished by the highest elements of life that are available and a humanity bordering on the divine appears. The devourer consumes the high thoughts and emotions of the consumed. Witness our divine Fat, who feed freely on their best fellow countrymen. Thus, living cannibalism is scientifically and morally sustained, and we contemplate sending out missionaries to inspire the derelict white races with it by and by. On this principle it is much more elevating to eat the philosophers, the poets, the musicians, and the inventors than to devour mere ordinary men, and to derive the greatest benefit they should certainly be eaten alive at the moment when engaged in their highest thinking.

Horroboo has an infinite knowledge of absoluteness. We
are glad to possess this information altho none of us has
the faintest conception what it means, for infinite thoughts
like the fat men's are not for finite minds, and since the
fat are always asleep they can never realize or impart what
they think.

"One prominent teaching alone we clearly comprehend,
namely, that God is like a fat man considerably magnified.
He has no feeling for the lean because he is not in the
least like them. He is at least four times as large as our
fattest. There were skeptics on this point until some two
thousand years ago when a revelation occurred. The lower
ribs on the left side of the fat suddenly gave way and
the stomach bulged forth gibbously about two feet in that
quarter; dyspepsia which had been due to stomach con-
striction then disappeared, the outer apertures in the stomachs closed up, for the digestive power had increased two
feet and was equal to all rational demands, and it was
recognized that after ten thousand years of virtuous suffering and struggle the fat were rewarded, adapted and
finished, which never could have been done except by a
god sufficiently like the fat to realize and sympathize with
their needs.

"Several circumstances thereupon improved astoundingly.
Things had reached a state where preparations were moving for voluntary tribal extinction by suicide, fat and lean,
feathered and featherless, suffering acutely and fiercely
disgusted with existence. We were diverted back to duty
by Providence, who on the very day that he expanded the
fat men laterally caused one of the featherless lean weighing sixty pounds to bring forward a plan which preserved
the tribe, restored happiness and has crowned us with that
illustrious superiority over other terrestrials which you
admire. The fat were about to erase themselves from
being on account of their dreadful wretchedness, the people

were gasping after annihilation because neither by diligence, virtue, prayerful flattery nor smiling chicanery could they force open the doors into the envied sphere of agony and fatness. On the verge of these final horrors it was proposed that a small aperture should be cut into that doleful precinct to permit the *principle* of the excluded commoner to pass in, while keeping the commoner himself out —mark, it was a commoner who proposed it: this reformer boldly alleged and advocated that of those who had no feathers certain carefully chosen individuals should be permitted under very delicate conditions to acquire them and to cross the sacred bar into the social tabernacle of the fetid felicities hitherto reserved for the fat men's children exclusively, saying plausibly that if the *principle* of equality without its reality were established, they would need be at no pains to go deeper for salvation. If we acknowledge the principle of the rights of men, why should they clamor for their rights too? We reasoned that enjoyment of the principle without the rights should satisfy them, and we found that it did."

CHAPTER XXVI

Horroboo Equality

"This renowned protocol of amity between the hunter bumpkins and the exalted caste of the saintly fat provided that every five years one from the lowly ranks should become fat to the extent of wearing feathers and eating or rotting food that would naturally supply a thousand, though his stomach could not be expected to swell through his ribs immediately nor all his diseases to arrive at once. By means of this generous concession, in one generation, which had then sunk down to twenty years, four persons would rise out of the lowly ranks of the mean and lean into the precious azure of corpulency and spirit, which would culminate in a glorious total of twenty emancipations in a brief hundred years. As a counterpoise to this noble grant the institution of carrying their fat lordships which you have seen in all its flaming grandeur was invented, lest the heads of the simple masses should be turned by their good fortune,—which is avoided by dividing the population into body-servants or carriers of the eminent, who are non-productive but are bathed in the odor of honor by proximity to its fountain, and common hunters, who never enjoy the perfume of grandeur and work twice as hard under the stress of collecting food for the carrier class as well as for themselves; but the sense that one out of them all in the term of five years will graduate from his humble sorrows, consoles and intoxicates them and they have many of the sensations reserved for the fat gods. Meanwhile the carrying has been of heroic benefit to the fat themselves by drawing them out of their palatial hole in the ground where for ten thousand years they had eaten in damp, moldy and majestic solitude, and diminishing the hours wherein they can exclusively eat.

"Now this just and redeeming fifth-year initiation into fatness was a flash of master genius, albeit struck out in the grimy mind of a crawling plebeian. It restored equality, in whose wake returned contentment, happiness and the soothing fusion of honied class-love. Amazing to think that for a hundred centuries society had been groaning heavily under inequality and had never learned this truly amazing secret of equality without its sting! How the tribe cursed its torpid forefathers for failing to devise the glittering necromancy earlier! Unequal equality now healed the sorry strifes and angry breaches of humanity."

I now addressed him: "Gorgeous Substance of the Sun, you appear to be speaking soberly, nor to be regaling me with the torrid scandals of African pleasantry, but here you have a tribe of fifty thousand soul-pods—for I do not think there is a true soul (in the theological seminary sense) in one of these shuffling shapes—of whom one hundred only belong to the order of shining corpulency, and four more that are admitted to that unblemished collection of abominations during man's lifetime—four out of fifty thousand may 'better their condition' in a generation, and this you call equality! Is this African wit?"

"Not so much wit as the highest kind of equality," he answered gravely. "Because any one in the tribe may be one of those fortunate four. A person who *may* become the greatest among us is surely equal to the greatest all the time—that ought to be logically clear to a mosquito."

"Perhaps," said I, "for seeing things wrong with cock logic is generally the logic of mosquito minds. But we are not mosquitoes, I hope, let us therefore examine. The 49,896 dust-motes of each generation who will never ascend to the honored position of fat men are equals of the fat because four out of their ranks become fat?"

"Absolutely equal, since all of the 49,896 have the same chance as the four."

"There is prodigious strength in your logic," said I, "to elevate so many with so little help, but I would gently submit a thought or two to Your Holy Infinitude. Those who are to become equal are not so until they have become, are they?"

He admitted this.

"Then those who never will become equal are neither now nor ever equal to their superiors?"

"It is quite true," said he.

"The fifty thousand minus four are never equals of the fat men, it seems."

"So it seems," cogitated his royal eminence, "but you forget that the whole tribe can be one of these four."

"Do you think that more than four can be four?" I asked. "Can four include fifty thousand?"

"Not precisely that," said he, very red under his ebony skin, "but all can join the race."

"But joining the race does not make all winners. You say that all are equal to the successful because all have an equal chance to run, but all have not an equal chance to win, and winning is what makes them equal to their superiors, who are the goal. Suppose it were decreed that all might run for fatness and *none* attain it, would you then assert that all were equal to the fat?"

"Emphatically not," said he; "how silly!"

"But they would all have an equal chance to run, which was your standard of equality, and the difference between none winning and four winning is ridiculously slight. And I will tell you why you are confused on this point, for I studied logic in connection with the ministry: logic would clarify the ministry of cant if their salaries were paid for their being logical. You imagine that all are equal, at least in opportunity, to the highest, because you do not happen to be able to select the destined four who will be equal; if you could select them and have the very individuals before your eyes it would be clear that all the residue of the fifty thousand are hopeless and permanent inferiors to whom the word equality in no way applies at any time. But they are a definite four and no others, there they are among the fifty thousand, living bodily without vagueness; the rest might as well be out of the race, for inequality and inferiority are their dark mortal doom."

"Why do you take such an interest in this?" he asked, sniffing suspiciously; "do you design to reason us out of our institutions?"

"By no means," I protested. "My motto is sweetness and light; I desire to give you light that you may know what wonderful institutions you have in order to be sweet while they destroy you. What are sweetness and light for but to make you reverently appreciative of the blessings you have tho they be few, and to keep you from making a fuss to get more?"

"If that is all," said he, his snuffles dying away and a bespeaking leer taking their place, "don't go to the trouble. Heavens! did you suppose that anyone, fat or mean, great or lank, imagines we have practical equality or desire it? Lord, no; it is theoretical equality we live on, sweetly the fat and full, and sourly the thin and hungry, but gladly all, for practical equality is a detestable idea to the low as well as the high, while theoretical equality is a constant banquet for the soul. The low are more jealous of their divine right to have and worship superiors than the high are of their right to spurn and despise their worshipers. But while it would be disgusting to have every clodhopper your practical equal it is elevating to consider him so in your mind. It generates in the brain the true constituent gases of love, which there firmly and safely corked propagate a thousand delightful little tinkling emotions that swell and fill the soul, circulating through it, proud, crabbed and exclusive though it be in reality, and invade it with a vapory decoction of sentiment so that every cell whirls about with a loosened ecstacy, stretched by the expansive power of the love gas to its tenderest distention, the cells all throbbing violently to quicken the love storm. This is what theoretical equality does for the lover by confining itself within the head. Now if this festal disturbance should escape from the walls of the mind and actually go out to hunt after the loved creatures to lavish itself upon them in the shape of practical equality and friendship, the strength of its compression in the head being removed, its sweet sensations would vanish away by volatile diffusion, and there would be no pleasure in equality. Practical love and equality are opposed to universal nature and are seductive agents of grief to humanity as a whole. Scientifically disciplined love has nothing to do with its objects; it is but a gaseous fermentation in a closed mental space for which purpose and its safe exercise the bones of the cranium have been implanted in man. He would be a thankless scalawag who should suffer these precious fumes to filter out and be lost in the air of common mankind, emptying the vault of his mind of all its emotional gems.

"The masses, I can tell you also, do not prize or wish this practical equality, for like their fat brethren their most pungent felicity is derived from loving generalities within the head. Whoever has a head can love an imaginary man; he possesses the stalwart faculty for generating love's fiery vapors toward some one a great distance off. The lean and starved usually select a fat gentleman as the target of their higher emotions, conscious that if they place their affections on things above, their souls will ever ascend toward the object. Theoretic equality, by which two leap the gap of caste in a decade, shows them that their aspirations are not hopeless; but practical equality, by placing them all on the sublime pinnacle of things at once, would rob them of high objects to strive for and reduce their natures to a barren emotionless calm. Equal love is like a drought. To secure a powerful activity of the affections you must project them upon some one higher or lower than yourself. The lower calls forth the pleasing exudations of pity, the higher fructifies the mighty ramifications of reverence; each prevents contact and pens the divine distillation in the cockles of the brain. Practical equality would pluck out the fragile fangs of tenderness. We achieve theoretical equality by the coronation of four new fat creatures every generation; practical equality would oblige us to open up the rich pastures of edible flesh to all human kind, and to allow all to eat."

"Here we have a man fitted for a high sphere in civilization, rusting at the head of a dirty African Empire!" I broke out impetuously, forgetting my deity attributes.

"America, with its flags, froth, fraud, jokes, starvation and embalmed specimens of extinct freedom, is the place for you, with your Ethiopian morals and powers. You would earn a glorious income in vanity and swag. And you could deposit your profits in the First National Bank of Isaac and Christ, which I intend to found and founder, where it will be safely kept until the latter's second coming, and you can return to Africa without fear of ever seeing it again. You are the soundest philosopher of this century and deserve a place with Tupper, Twangle, Eddy, Tingley, Twinkle, Besant and Blavatsky. You are a true saint, a second Buddha, who ought to go into business as a manufacturer of Messiahs of Equality."

The leader of men replied blushing: "But you don't fathom my ambition, Serenity; I am a literary genius, and I want to have my Horroboo writings translated to the world so that I may dazzle all mankind as I have blinded my nation with them at home. My literary method is chaste and up-to-date. I use literature as the art of picking out microscopic granules of pleasure from the common mire of human experience, sticking them together in a dough of sparkling sprightly words, and giving the product to the public as an accurate specimen of human life, to promote contentment with poverty. I hold that an author who cannot tickle the ribs of laughter to convince his readers that bad is good, and misery a divine thing for the majority, is no better than a literary cow. He must close his eyes to the realities of the world and sift out as many little grains of brightness from the general woe as he can find. If none can be found he must invent some. Then let him glue them together in an esthetic mush of adhesive grammar, and sugar all with optimism to anodyne the multitude. I have dazed and enchanted the whole Horroboo tribe and established literature as a deadly power to strangle truth, by following these tenets of literary creation, and I think I can strangle the rest of the world with them."

His eyes were set with devouring eagerness as he uttered these radiant words, and from the depth of my soul my answer came

"Griffelak, for the discovery of these deep laws you are entitled to an early grave in Westminster Abbey, while your foul soul floats friendless in the dizzy dome of the universe. You deserve an imperishable rocking-chair at the first lunch counter of civilized letters. With humor you can chortle through the abysses of human injustice, iniquity and wrong, seeing nothing. You can sweeten life for all robbed and outraged sufferers by telling them they are not suffering; and to all the creators of their suffering you can bring heaven's own peace by singing in poetry that all their victims are more blest for being ruined. Here is my hand, old pirate, I will translate your books."

As a hungry lion caresses his keeper for meat, or an affectionate dog licks the skin of his master, so Griffelak kissed my fingers a thousand times and would have applied the same fondness to my face if I had not reminded him that sentiment and business had long since been divorced and marriage between them abolished, and that we still had things commercially profitable to talk about.

"To resume, I will take you on a circuit of civilization to conciliate workingmen with their lot. Our workingmen, blessed little gullibles, are making trouble on account of their imaginary degradation; and they are such excellent objects of your kind of love—if rich people only knew the theory—that love would be immediately generated in great quantities, causing the workingmen to recover from the distemper they are in from not understanding that they are really equal in your way to everybody else. 'Unequal Equality' is the amalgamating formula. The poor devils' ignorance must be buttered thick with it; we will carry it to the workshops and sweatshops. And when your silvery solo is heard, there will be massive contributions from the wealthy to the cause of Equal Inequality."

"I will go wherever you wish," said Griffelak, "for I am an apostle of light if the salary is what it should be. I would even preach in a Fifth Avenue church."

I replied, patting him on the back:

"That savory discrimination of love in the head from love in the world deserves a pope's diadem and a trust potentate's salary, and certainly will be as epoch-making in the sphere of factories and enlarged grave-yards as Darwin's beautiful introduction of us to our ancestors was for a time a storm-maker in ecclesiastical tea-parties."

CHAPTER XXVII

I Meet the Fat

The lecture contract being ratified and a brief sleep taken, with a lunch of baked human possibilities, we returned to the subject of institutions. "Tell me," said I, "how it is that the four who are to be honored with fat are selected."

"By an honest competition of worthiness," he answered. "Every five years we have a rivalry of the whole tribe to ascertain who can longest abstain from eating; the victor in the greatest number of these noble trials is the happy Horroboo who is elevated to the proprietorship of feathers and fat; if there is a tie among several a separate contest is held to decide."

"I fail to see how this sheds light upon the virtue of the contestants, or upon their fitness for the exalted station of fatmen."

"It is not supposed to show their virtue or fitness for anything, for virtue has no connection with fatness or examinations; but you must have some standard of human promotion and provided it is severe enough I don't see that it makes much difference what the criterion is. Some were in favor of making it the amount of vinegar a man could drink, others the period he could stand on his head, yet others the number of loose and disconnected sounds he could fasten longitudinally in his memory, a few even contended that the surest test would be to select the man who could hang longest by the neck without dying, but at length all agreed that fasting was best, since a man capable of starving himself soundly must surely have a pat ability for starving others, which is a power fat men must continually exercise.

"The equality revolution I have described brought the feather-men not only better health but a new tranquillity of mind. No longer in fear of bodily molestation they abandoned their occasional moments between eatings to sleep, and even taught themselves to eat and sleep at the same time. During recent centuries they have seldom awakened to full consciousness and it is known that they have clean lost a bundle of feelings and intellectual powers belonging to the herd and marking their vulgarity: for example, they show no sympathy for others under any conditions and the range of their ideas is limited to the two processes of eating and preventing others from doing so."

I exclaimed, horrified: "Do you tell me that others of your tribe hanker to become the counterparts of these dismal mentally and morally eviscerated diseased congenital idiots?"

"All of them do; it is a sure evidence of refinement to lose a natural impulse or a feeling or an ability to think: altho one may never be a fatman himself, to be like them is the nearest thing to complete Horroboo culture."

"Your Imperial Highness," I cried, struck by an inquisitive idea, "I should like to talk with some of these distinguished beings."

"Talk with them? Gladly, they are always happy to
talk."

"But tell me one thing first that I may not make myself
ridiculous. Besides the servants bearing their excellencies
I notice under each frame the impressive figure of a man
walking; his head and shoulders are horizontally bowed
because he cannot go erect underneath: what is he?—the
physician to their sick highnesses? or their scavenger? or
errand-boy? and why does he not walk outside where he
can hold up his head?"

"Those are the Counsellors," answered Emperor Griffelak. "The stooped position in which you remark them is
their natural one. Having stood and walked in that folded
attitude for many thousand years they have grown so,
and now are born bent and curved; nor are they allowed
to walk except where you see them, lest striving to
straighten their necks they should forget the reverence
due the masters lying above them, on whom their thoughts
must be exclusively intent."

"Select the fattest, Your Puissance," I requested; "I may
be able to get more out of them."

Griffelak signalled a group bearing a brace of fabulous
rotundities to approach and deposit their load of sleep upon
the earth. The recumbent hillocks did not stir and I could
canvass their topography without impertinence. They were
about six feet in length and fourteen in breadth and thick-
ness, for certainly as they lay on their backs the perihelion
of their stomachs was not short of fourteen feet from the
ground, nor was the circumference of the man's leg by
actual measurement, which I took near the thigh, an inch
less than eleven feet ten. The head on the contrary was
about half the normal size, indicating the disappearance

of faculties, which even the cranium stomach had not entirely made good.

"Wake them," I said.

Griffelak spoke a few words to the fifty attendants of the serene sleepers, who vigorously seized on them and rolled them up and down the avenue the space of a hundred feet, then kneaded and thumped their flesh, and lastly held them upside down to concentrate some blood into their heads. This treatment finally elicited a few groans to signify that their consciousness was approaching.

I addressed them very civilly, saying that I should enjoy their companionship in travel for the benefit of science and the enlightenment of the twilight places of the earth where they were unknown, to which they discourteously replied by merely opening their mouths to the breadth of a fissure that obliterated the other features and suggested a crevice in eternity on account of the awful things below, whereupon a couple of attendants sprang forward with bags and began to fill the openings with choice carvings of raw flesh and live pigs, frogs and toads. Here was the visual typification of their belief that live things must be eaten alive to transfer the principle of life to the eater. They also swallowed many animals whole to avoil impairment of the life principle in its passage from the original owner to them. The size of the life thus swallowed was a ponderous item of their dietetics, whence they were all too often choked in the sturdy effort to force down souls too wide for their gullets. In the nick of their odious discourtesy a voice which might have emanated from the entrails of the mammoths began to speak and I perceived the lips of the counsellor in motion, who replied without looking up from his feet in these words:

"We consent to be pleased by your celestial offer, we even deign to flatter Your Godliness with a reply: nevertheless we must decline. Where could we find the institution of sleep so enterically established as here? Where else are grateful multitudes candidly deprived of these bounteous carloads of food which no one eats? In what clime is commerce so fearfully appreciated and humanity so divinely depreciated? God knows, nowhere. We have free libraries and free lead: free books for the empty brain and free bullets for the empty body. Politely pardon us therefore if we say that your offer of heaven is a little stale. This is heaven. Do you realize the pleasure of being shot? Learn it, for you will not then boast idly to us of the dazzling advantages of public lectures in foreign lands: we have blessings which ye know not of and we prefer to disseminate them at home. Mankind here has long since left the zenith of perfection below. Our fat is the symbol of equal privilege—all are equally entitled to look at it. None are debarred from becoming like us; we have solved the social troubles of mankind by delightful variety of stimulating social grades upon a groundwork of indestructible equality of fancy. Besides we have equality of dreams. Think of it! Every man is freely permitted to dream what he pleases! Who could ever do that before? All are equal to us except in appearance and reality; all own equal property with us save in the faint details of feathers and food, our only values here, which we, the worthy fat parasites, retain exclusively for the general good."

The slick fellow said much more in the same strain, glibly and unctuously as if he had it by heart, never looking away from his toes. I turned to the Emperor for explanation.

"It is the fat gentleman speaking through the tongue of his Counsellor," said His Majesty. "Thinking on politically dangerous and heterodox subjects, by which I mean those foreign to the monopoly of food, was many thousand years ago found to be incompatible with the accumulation of fat;

to relieve our fat prophets of this delay in their mission by lifting the drag of thinking from their intestinal vitality, the cleverest brains of the tribe were selected and set apart for their use. These Counsellors are not separate entities or individuals as you might suspect from the circumstance of their living in separate bodies, they are a section of the fat drones divided off by moral fission as a physical annex for the deposition of the fatmen's brains. You notice they speak in the first person, they recognize themselves as the mental essence of the parent stock. It is a beautiful case of division of labor, transferred function, absolute identity of one person in two bodies, a mysterious compound problem of chemical psychology, our famous unsolved surprise of spirit oneness with spatial twoness."

"But haven't the fat gentry something to say for themselves?" I persisted.

"They have given over learning to talk. It is a great and wasting exertion, contumelious to fatness, in which they do not need to engage since everything even to thinking and talking is better done for them by experts; it nourishes friction in the brain and its utility for personages of high birth and large estate is problematical; enough to say it takes off flesh."

I was studying the physignomy of the curved varlet. He looked his part wonderfully, you were sure he was somebody beside himself: a shadowy furtive clairvoyant face, wild wavering legal eye, hair long, lank, straight and tousled, for all the world an international statue of Forensic Solemnity. From appearances he might have been a police judge, a county shyster, or a Supreme Justice of the nation. On my making a tour of inspection around his eager slimness some unexpected traits of his character disclosed themselves; as I turned his various corners new individuals seemed abruptly to stand forth in his nude

essence: in spite of his courageous all-but nakedness, I
was at one instant morally certain that I saw a French-
man, after the next curve in my path it was a German,
then an Englishman, later a Russian, and the last of his
facets was indisputably Yankee.   In deep bewilderment
I traced my course around him a second time only to discover the same unprecedented reflections produced in the
same order.   While I stood mopping by brow and battling
with the gurgling billows of my amazement, the complex
object began to speak again, droning his words out downward and dolefully; my traveling proposition was still on
his mind:

"To leave our country would be cruelly unjust to our
countrymen, for fat is a dropsical hindrance to those who
must work, and now, as it has pleased God that all but
ourselves shall ceaselessly work, how great would their
burden of suffering be if above the weight of their toil
they were constrained to carry that of fat also!   We came
to their rescue and divided the labor: we carry the fat
and they the toil, we dedicate and surrender our bodies
a sleeping sacrifice to bear the cross of all the people's fat
and rescue the workers from the desperate weight of that
curse.   We are somewhat assisted in carrying this fat by
those who carry us, but you must remember that their
exertion is noble, since like us they support fat, and their
effort in doing it is not to be compared with ours, for
while they sustain the same quantity of fat that we do,
there are fifty of them to uphold upon these poles the
burden which only two of us are obliged to maintain upon
our bones.   We also redeem the tribe from the toilsome strain
of eating food by eating it for them; we deliver them from
the dangers to life incident to taking foreign substances
into the system through the mouth, which exceed the infinite.   We give our inner substance to the conjugal teeth
of microbes to preserve our countrymen from their inju-
dicious lacerations.   We cannot abandon our country."

I availed to hold my sides together and keep my latent explosions limited to facial athletics and wrinkled roars, and eventually straightened myself to inquire from whence he derived his thoughts.

"I never rest from recognizing that I am His Worship," he answered, pointing to the drooping tun of avoirdupois; "I have no self and therefore no mind of my own, for I could not store it in this borrowed body; my thoughts come to me out of that vast thinker's fat brain, which is my superliminal mind."

The Emperor came again to relieve my perplexity. "They all look like this one and you never could guess how it is done. When they are very young and before it has grown to much size, so that the operation is safe, we take their wills out through a slight incision in the skull. The bone heals and all appears as before. The thinking power remains intact, in truth is strangely facilitated and augmented in its growth by concentration of all cerebral nutriment in itself with no food waste on volition; bereft of voluntary force they readily accept all ideas that come from authority, and being taught from infancy that they are the personality of the fat men they believe it with inexpugnable conviction; and they grow marvelously clever and cunning, but all for the benefit of the fat, whom, regarding as themselves, they worship with violent infatuation. It is absolute selfishness unconsciously turned to absolutely altruistic uses: they serve the State in the persons of the Fat, while imagining that it is solely themselves they are exalting."

I questioned him if they had no other function.

"Yes, numerous ones: they amuse us with songs of their invention praising the Gluttons and their wisdom; they contrive long harangues for delivery in public places showing the matchless worth of our Horroboo breed above the rest of created creatures, which, they derisively avouch, are foaled, not born; whenever a citizen grows discontented during a famine occasioned by the fat men's feelings they prove from the language of the bark of trees, legible to none but them, that it is the will of the Great Spirit to have a period of popular starvation; they are the instructors of the young in what pertains to a useful life—that is, in the mythology of lost Ethiopian tribes and the supposed shape of their larynx in the pronunciation of words, with photographs of the impressions they left on the air, the language of Adam as reconstructed from the beats of a perfect man's heart after death, the places sat upon by extinct thinkers, whether prophets were first made of smoke or sorrow, the bearing of fingernails on the roots of trees, the moral character of the departed as shown by the longitudinal texture of their disappointed bones, the obligation of obedience to the grandparents of our first grandparents in all untried emergencies to come, to save the mind from wearing out, the universal history of feathers, ditto of fat, ditto of vacuums, a study of the life of Griffelak I. to form the morals of the young, the location on the first goose of the feathers transmitted to the present first families as they lie on these litters, dictated from the memory of a band of young rememberers trained to recall the past by looking eighteen hours a day into graves, a microscopic analysis of the dried skins of first families for emulation, the mystery of the qualities of fatness, the holiness of the undiscovered, the heavenly beauty of earthly ugliness and vice versa, the relation of entrails to eternity, and a number of other pithecoid problems upon which our public school system turns its glassy eye."

CHAPTER XXVIII

The Food Inclosures

It was now declining toward the cool of the afternoon and we took our way to the food inclosures. They were in a circle of the city set apart for them, quite central, so that at all times but especially during famines the people might have the quantities of collected and forbidden food under their eyes. They were thus disciplined to self-control, a sense of the awful nearness of death, and respect for the awfuler rights of property. The decaying nutriment would send its fumes far and wide, proving to each slowly dying abstainer the beauty and holiness of firmly starving in an ocean of food.

About these inclosures ethics abounded. Every man cared more for his principles than for his constitution; here all lived for the pure idea in opposition to the sordidness of nutrition; food was despised and dreaded as material; a righteous skeleton was more honored than a heart corrupted by lusting after bread and milk; their pious precept was that God had special heavenly mansions for such skeletons; they held it evil to preserve life against the sound religion of submission to law; faith in God was medically declared to be more physically strengthening (for the poor) than beefsteak, and cheaper; if any food besides Faith in God was needed by the poor, a potato was recommended; might for the first time politely groveled to right before grinding it to atoms. Who among these skyward-starving saints would care to hang paving-stones to his soul by snatching a knob of flesh from legal and orderly decay to increase the tears of his life? Who would steal a criminal bone in the presence of the frowning God in the Fat? Who would jeopardize his religious notions and ethical foundations and practical rules and principal corollaries, for nothing but vile happiness on a mean globule of transitory matter spinning forever through an idle void? No true Horroboo would stoop so low; the teaching of his Sunday School had saved him from that; Eternity was always present in their eyes, tho nothing was present in their stomachs. It was a Horroboo proverb that when a man was very hungry he had eaten God, which made hunger the essence of their worship. The Fat had composed this proverb, but they had never eaten God.

The inclosures were formed by a low fencework of interwoven brush reaching about to the neck of an average man but transparent to small women and children through the interstices; over the meshed gate of each was the owner's name in fancy lithograph; and their size varied according to the number of goose feathers the owner's first ancestor had been entitled to wear. The amount of food the nabob could own and rot increased directly with the size of his title to these goose feathers.

Despite my respect for the ethical verities I could not help exclaiming, "If this is where the unused carcasses are thrown I should think the famished people would jump in and snatch them."

"Not for this world and a handsome load of interest-bearing bonds on heaven! They would feel themselves dishonored forever and foresee their dead souls moaning through infinite spacelessness clad in a rancid pall. Whatever may be their outward appearance as to cleanliness and intellect, our people are developed to a very delicate altitude morally; they are like reverent lobsters in a boiling kettle with the lid of conscience on—under that lid they are well contented to stew or fry, asking no reasons for the heat consuming them if they can see that reassuring cover through the steam. Three deaths a day to each of them, spiced with torture and vivisection, could not goad them to pluck a bone through these hallowed twigs."

I summed the matter up to His Horroboo Highness as I thus far understood it and asked him if I was right. I said: "These fleshy persons, Their Royal Fatnesses, are in possession of the entire sustenance of the tribe, to give or withhold as they feel moved; they cause measureless quantities of food to be wasted, of which their fellow tribesmen are in perishing need, with no cause but the chance occasional turbulence of their comatose corpulency; and they are not only useless and most of the time asleep, being nothing but a great sewer upon society carrying everything good off to ruin and waste and leaving depletion and wretchedness worse than ten battle-fields, but they are utterly powerless both in mind and body to protect and enforce their spurious fantastical claims: and yet your mighty nation of fifty thousand quasi souls suffers and submits to them; and to crest all, or rather to load all with unimaginable infamy, these hundred bladders of senseless grease are not human, for the normal faculties and sympathies of men are dead in them, having been absorbed and transmuted into eating and fat; and finally though they are a colossal deception openly and visibly, and so decayed and imbecile that they cannot support the fraud by any thought or act of their own, others, these spineless counsellors and slaves, are employed to carry on the shameless hoax for them, and the people revel in the murderous lie which they inflict upon themselves. It is as if the nation revered a hundred moribund sheep or swine and appointed them to be owners of their food sources and the gods of their life."

"You learn like a god yourself, and testify your immaculate descension," Milto and Griffelak simultaneously roared.

"Thank you, I deserve no credit; for the moment I felt myself back in civilization attending a directors' meeting, and I think I was dreaming when I spoke; if you have any other equally progressive institutions to show off let us see them at once."

"After coffee," they said, "we have afternoon coffee now.'

In a cheerful spot with ripe bananas hanging over our heads and brilliant flowers garnishing the lawns of shaven grass, with brooklets rippling musically past our feet and shady dells inviting the listener with divine notes of native birds concealed in their airy aisles, we drank the steaming liquid which sable servants brought in a shining samovar. The cups were of the usual size and carved from ivory, the sugar was as sweet as any I have tasted, and the wine jelly proudly transfused a most ancient suggestion. We also smoked, for by this time I had circulated the cosy habit, tilting our chairs against the trees companionably, while exchanging a few white and black anecdotes in a conversational tone. The mocha thawed the vitals of Griffelak and under its genial effluence he reached beneath the table and drew out a bottle. We clicked our ivories and drank. It was ambrosia, for no liquor in civilization compares with it. I imbibed sparingly, as interviewing two kings, and had no intention of spoiling a choice bit of news through drunkenness.

"Is this a popular drink?" I inquired. "If so I could readily enthrall myself among your lower classes! it is a heavenly beverage in which I have already counted numerous godlike flavors."

"We do not waste this on the common trash," replied my royal friend.

At this moment the fat men's procession filed somberly across the noble esplanade, visible through the spaces of the trees. Every soul of them had the neck of a skin bag in his mouth which he was sucking with great fury, about two gallons in size.

"This is their drinking time," commented Griffelak, tapping his bottle: "the same, ambrosia do you call it? nepenthe in our syntax; they drink two gallons each at this hour and four at bed-time to drown their sorrow for the poor starving people whose woe gnaws them to the quick with a bitter muriatic. anguish. They suffer sorely because it is against the laws of the Cosmos buried in their abdomens to give the sufferers food, whence they keep themselves in a state of intoxication day and night to be unconscious of the misery they are compelled by the Order and Avarice of the Universe to inflict."

"What do the popular dregs drink?" I queried, thinking I might learn something for the cause of temperance at home.

He drew on a long face and spoke as it were from a new-made grave. "Ah, Sir, this is the whole trouble with the populace class—they drink. God save me from speaking ill of my countrymen, but they are addicted to their cups: they have a spirit composed of ninety-nine parts rain-water and one sulphuric acid with which they ravish their vitals weekly; it keeps them poor; it is manufactured by command of the fat men and sold to the people at a prodigious profit, one per cent. of which is given to free lectures on astronomy. Were it not for these astronomical lectures the traffic might be abolished, for none are more opposed to this damning drink habit in the masses than the fat, but what would the common people know about the stars if this free learning were interdicted by the abolition of inebriousness? The Fat also give a thousandth of one per cent of their drink profit to support addresses on the evils of intemperance and if the manufacture of liquor and drinking were stopped these discourses would have to collapse for want of funds, our war against the sin of drink would then have to cease, the consumption of intoxicants would multiply ten times and the working people would be lying dead drunk in one spirituous heap the year long. The Fat Absolutes often earnestly expostulate with them, through the medium of their delegated brains, upon

the wickedness of drinking up their substance, and it is
fortunate for them that they have not as much food as
they have drink for they would be as great gluttons as they
are tipplers and sots if they could. Gluttony as opposed
to the genius and piety of our nation is much spoken against
by the Counsellors under command of their broad-bellied
patrons. The Gorgers have a series of annual frowns
which they exhibit at evening meetings in the fall to dis-
suade the people from giving a loose rein to their carnal
appetites.

"Now," concluded Griffelak, with the supersolid infinite-
ness of a university philosophy-doctor in his manner, "I
have proved by the foregoing chain of arguments that the
unbridled lust for liquor which throbs like a cruel demon
in the alcoholic marrow of our rabble is the cause of their
dreadful indigence and ruin. If it wasn't for the profit that
we make on the liquor, drunkenness would end. We pray
for this continually, the fat and I, and are careful to see
that our prayers are not answered. Should this transpire
the fat would give them as much less food as they now
spend for drink, which would keep the same profit in the
corpulent coffers without wandering out to the people and
back—but there would be less business activity and fewer
lost souls to establish the prophesied frailty of human
nature. We have to guard that frailty with great scruple
to protect the credit of the prophets. The tendency to
gluttony from which the Horroboo herd now suffer unconsciously, their stomachs and morals being much broken
down by it without their knowledge, would be corrected
by the shrinkage of their affluence, however, and the food
of the many now squandered on drink could be saved by
the fat men to invest in their inclosures."

CHAPTER XXIX

Pillars of the Horroboo State

This eloquent view of the temperance question being new to me I hazarded no comment and we walked arm in arm to the locality of another leading Horroboo institution. It was one of the grand metropolitan circles, whither I perceived from a distance that we had been preceded by the first citizens. Here and there were corpses in various grades of decomposition by whose sides lay stretched out the fat dotards on the customary support of their backs. The stench was the familiar mephitic one of decayed humanity, but of titan texture; I refused to go further when I saw the odorous cause and examined the deadly position with my field glasses.

"In heaven's name, what does this portend?" gasped I through my handkerchief.

"These bodies are the spoils and perils of our last war," gurgled Griffelak, inhaling a luxurious breath. "Of course like all other nourishment they belong to the well-bellied proprietors. After the possession of a feather and the inflated stomach the highest dignity is to possess a body killed in battle. The Fatmen do not wish to eat them, for the honor of owning what others have not would then vanish, so they convene here every afternoon and occupy the remains until the softening carrion has evaporated entirely away. The distinction of owning these cadavers is twofold: human flesh of foreigners is the prime delicacy of all seasons to the tribal palate, all long with florid but restrained savage propriety to feel a morsel of this cloying nutriment between their molars, which the Fat deny themselves and forbid to others with an elegant sense of patrician exclusiveness; it is also considered an act of fine prowess to kill an enemy, which the fat alone are worthy

to perform (albeit quite unable to do so), and the theory
is that the fat men are the doughty slayers of all the bodies
that are brought in from battle, altho they always take to
their beds and remain there with their heads under cover
counting their feathers while the others sally forth to fight.
Pictures are painted of the fat giants fiercely seated on
snorting elephants with flames of fire darting from their
eyes, and killing thousands of their enemies with a blast-
ing look, and the rustic hinds of the tribe who have done
all the fighting there was, abase themselves before these
glorious photographs, worshiping the bravery of their superiors' pictures and hopelessly praying that they may sometime themselves become valorous.

"Sitting thus on decomposing flesh causes fevers and
sudden deaths among the fat veterans, but they murmur
not at the blows of destiny if they can maintain the honor
of their position by the sacrifice of their lives, especially
as their mental powers are insufficient to associate sickness and rot together. Besides, to see their tribesmen
feasting on these dainty corpses would engender greater
mortality among them."

"Disgusting!" said I in English, and the two potentates
thought I was praising them in celestial and clapped their
hands.

"By breeding the fat together patiently," confided Griffelak, "we hope to get a species four times larger. It will
be an unprecedented consolation. The fatter you are the
more room you have for fat if you always put it on the
outside. We are a pretty proud nation now, for we invented
this idea of the repeated combination of great personalities until everything great is under one head, but if our
personal geniuses should swell two or three times in extent,
the small people would go to pieces with their arrogant
haughtiness at having reared up such hitherto unattainable
splendors."

Milto, however, had grown sober and stern listening to his friend's account of things and he now spoke: "If we had those bloated beasts in our habitation we should eat them in short space and get them out of the way to have our own food without their pampered pretension to interference."

Griffelak shrunk into half of himself with groans of mortal terror. "Hush!!" he simpered. "If a Horroboo should hear such baleful words the liberties of the people and my ancient throne would be smashed! If that heinous sentiment pierced through the mailed prejudice of a single mind here it would be fatal to every precious thing that exists under the smiling bloodstained shackles of my government! Let them once imbibe the fallacy that they could eat these hideous whales—which in secret I confess they are—and they would do it in defiance of our lying Seventy-Thousand-Year-Old-Book, the teachings of Counsellors, or the clubs of my Brain-Breakers,—and logic, religion, high-feeding and faith would die out of the world; we should become a prey to devils and general nourishment; Hades, pandemonium and happiness would possess the earth; the sin of general justice would foam over the planet! No! We keep up the embalmed edifice of society by a balance of powers: the fat are balanced on the backs of the people that carry them, these are balanced on the necks of the people that feed them both, and I and the Counsellors balance this whole three-storied human cathedral by distributing ourselves around its side walls and seizing on to anything we can get for support. The fatmen thus sustain me and teach the people below by the immense weight of their prestige that I am their indispensable protector; if I said this alone, unbuttressed by a vast capital of fat, the people would regard it as a self-interested statement and throw me off. I respond by treating the Gluttons with all the reverend punctilio of a clerk and assuring the people that the entire fabric of popular happiness stands on feathers and fat, tho of course I know that these corpulent beasts have been absolute fools these ten thousand years. Still, they are the prop of my throne, my very existence as an Emperor depends on their wink, and I can't give them up. The counsellors, being easily shuffled and moved about and elastically fitting into any hole, preserve the equilibrium of the balance. Of course these demented tumors take themselves seriously, so far as a ray of consciousness ever penetrates their putrid bulks, but those shrewd fellows the counsellors, although wanting in the power or desire to interfere, and fancying themselves with one lobe of the brain identical with their masters' brains, see through it all with the other lobe: they know what a fraud I am and what a stupendous fable these shapeless oil tanks are, but they are wedded to their position as one of fame and honor, altho it is the most infamously servile one in the state. The expurgation of their wills in childhood deprived them of the force to realize a condition of servility and they are never so flattered as when a fat man slaps them. They then jump about him like a pet fawn and kiss him wherever they can and the more rapidly the blows fall about their ears the more thickly they slaver on the kisses."

"I should like to be taught that process of will chirurgery," I interrupted, "for I rank it from your account as the best spiritual anaesthetic; it would relieve servants high and low, as well as indigent educated gentlemen with mind who live by professing character, from all sensitiveness to humiliation; there are countries where it would be an untold blessing and a due ballast on the antics of aspiration. It would save our professors and clergymen from some mysterious mortifications. It seems to be the complete welding of thought and dollar to which all fine forces of civilization tend, yet have not absolutely attained."

"You shall be taught the art," rejoined Griffelak graciously. "It effects the euthanasia of the moral nature in its germ, leaving the mind a highly sharpened thinking machine devoid of moral impulse or perception."

"Capital!" I observed; "it is the very discovery the learned world has been seeking these many centuries, and to think it should have been dormant here in these musty wilds for twelve thousand yawning years!"

"As I was saying," Griffelak resumed, "the counsellors do their share of keeping up our splendid system because they derive huge enjoyment from walking curved over beneath their masters, and because they secretly imagine that the whole fabric of state rests on them, from the power of their eloquence to keep the people in the slavish path. Their crooked spines are to them a badge of the mighty affairs of the community which they carry. They are quite contented with these austere rewards and ask nothing more. Their food is the skins and claws of the animals which the fat men eat, plentiful such as they are, but a little dry. When a fat patron dies his Counsellor is respectfully burned alive to accentuate the identity; also because he may need his brains in the next world. The Counsellors live in a circle by themselves, indulging no intercourse with the hunter caste, whom they consider dogs because their spines are not curved. If you observe you will notice that they never lift their eyes from their own feet, for which they feel an electric veneration compounded of esthetics and religion; none of them has ever seen the sky, it would be an infallible pollution, expiable only by twelve days of diet on unseasoned hair. The last of their kind who ventured to look at the sky became blind with horror at the evil possibilities that he saw in it. This was three thousand years ago. They are now providentially aided in resisting the temptation to look upward by the lost use of the muscles that revolve and raise the head, which have atrophied in such a degree that if one of them designed to catch a glimpse of the heavenly vault he would be obliged to lie upon the bend of his neck and shoulders with his feet elevated against a wall."

Just then a common Horroboo passed with a feather about an inch long fastened to his loin-cloth and the upper part of him confined in a species of cage which brought the higher links of his neckbone and his head into the rainbow shape of the counsellors and held them there fast.

"What does this mean?" I queried nervously; "I thought feather-wearing was now limited to the abdominous giants; is this strange object getting up a revolution?"

"He is a dangerous character," answered Griffelak. "He is a common food-digger who has somehow acquired the power to think. This renders him foully pernicious to the commonwealth since his back is neither bent fixed nor his will extracted. He might communicate his thoughts to others and topple the empire down. To avert this crisis we bribe him in the delicate manner that you see. He is honored with the privilege of wearing a pin-feather one hour a fortnight, and is put in training for the proud position of Counsellor by that cage, which is training his head down to the right angle. The counsellors are also teaching him to read the bark of trees, which must always be done in a closed space under ground, for otherwise the language refuses to appear."

"Have you lamps?"

He scratched his head, and I defined lamps.

"Oh, no, light would dim the meaning, it has to be done in the dark."

"Poor wretch! doesn't he suffer in that brutal cage?"

"Horribly, but he is happy. He can never be a counsellor himself because he still has a will, but that is to be taken out of his children, who, if they inherit his thinking genius, will be full-fledged counsellors, if not they will hungrily hunt. He has to associate with the common flesh-catchers all his life, but they stand in painful awe of him by reason of his cage and feather, and on his part he considers them a community of worms, he speaks to them only when he must, in terms of insolent hate, he bitterly reproaches them for polluting the sphere with their existence tho he was yesterday one of them in all points and is to-day no better, but worse in undergoing a thousand tortures to accomplish the mutilation of his children. He proudly bears his griefs and sores, chewing the sour cud of expectation that his children will be found worthy to become spiritual eunuchs. And he never tells the people his thoughts. By cage and feather and pride he is converted into a sepulcher of the light of his soul; being a thinker he was divinely intended to lead his brethren out of bondage, but a cruel cage and a pin-feather badge purchase and persuade his mind and quell his manly stirrings eternally. This nobly simple arrangement has preserved the State from overthrow unnumbered times.

"Man is governed by invisible soapbubbles; we did not know that formerly and resorted to force, which kindled his wrath: we were in jeopardy and invented the inscrutable soapbubble; ocean froth does excellently well only it is too real, being impregnated with salt; uncompressed steam, if it has vanished, does the work, or a man's breath if it is ten centuries old; the imprint of a faded memory is cogent, not less so the smoke of the first fire ever kindled; other powers being absent the collected friction of the original star-dust answers, or even the dreams of Eve before she was removed from Adam; I have known the sentiment that evaporated from a drop of rain that never fell to light up destructive emotion in a mob; you can keep men from taking what is theirs by daily doses of the colors of prehistoric rainbows; another infallible remedy is porous emptiness buried in the center of the earth in the surviving pods of languages that were never spoken, inhaled at one o'clock nightly through a long tube. With all these agencies at command to carry on government and keep the poor people loyal to canned dreams we seldom call in the whipping post or harpoon."

"It can't be that all who stumble on the ability to think will perjure and sell themselves for these full-feigned fripperies!" I declared; "you must have some occult method of heading off potent inflammations and insurrections."

The swarthy monarchs twinkled their protuberant eyes at each other luminously. "Let us tell him," said Milto, and the Horroboo proceeded as follows:

"Now and then a hunter learns to think who will not sell himself to us. He nurses in solemn wrath his criminal purpose to speak the unmangled truth to his compeers. He resists the gallant feather and syren cage, the bubbles, rainbows and departed smell of precosmic smoke, and goes about uttering vainglorious calumnies against visceral dignitaries and my just rule. We prefer not to make a public example of these misguided rebels against the harmonious perfection of our social miracle, and thus to nail them into the arching blue of martyrdom and advertise their miscreant social creed and murderous names. Their well-known self-centered motive in posing as friends of men is a sordid desire for notoriety; as one of our Counsellors has said in a faculty meeting: 'They crave notoriety at any cost, for some men prefer to be prominent on the wrong side of any given issue, rather than to be unrecognized on the right,' of whom in general we may specify one Socrates and another Jesus, notorious characters in their day who did not belong to our tribe, and who have been too freely advertised considering how they were disposed of by their contemporaries; the less said about them the better, and the former was allowed to live too long before they brought his notoriety to the hemlock:—they should have kept the latter alive reforming Jerusalem in connection with practical philanthropists, to emasculate his enthusiasm, if they had wished to throttle his heresy; let others heed and take warning and reflect on the untimely consequences of unpopularity. 'Martyrdom perpetuates pernicious creeds,' says an ex-hangman living in retirement.

"We therefore incubate a war in our communal coops to extirpate the heretics and calm the frenzies. There has been a perpetual dual alliance for this purpose between King Milto's ancestors and mine against our subjects through misty generations back, only known to the dead and ourselves. If one of us has trouble with domestic affairs he telephones the other to begin a war on his outskirts and makes the welkin ring with the iniquity of the invading Rinyo or Ourselves, our domestic complaints are snuffed out by inarticulate alien rage, our pestilent thinkers turn their thoughts to the extinction of foreigners, which is the only state-recognized object of thinking at all times; prophets, philosophers and saints on each side of the bloody dividing ditch have now no thought above the hallowed carnage of their opponent vermin (also saints, philosophers and prophets at home), pulpit doors are nailed up and laboratories cease from sighing, college presidents beat their pens into bullets and their brains into syndicate shares, all send the common people forth to battle for the Lord, and thirst to have their neighbors die bravely to leave a glorious reputation and some property, we put the fat men to bed, the dangerous thinkers in the front rank and the generals in the rear, Milto and I retire to distant elevations behind our troops respectively to direct operations: at the end of the battle, which we craftily convert into a draw to preserve the balance of power as natural friends and allies must, we find our nations purged of the bloody villains who threatened government, gluttons and culture with thought, and we return to our homes with neither heretics nor their incendiary doctrines to mar our repose or stimulate our subjects' appetites. And I can assure you that this is a better way of wiping out schisms than your ecclesiastical autos-da-fé, for the schismatics here wipe themselves out to the bray of horns and think they are saving their country."

I felt that we had done a large day's work and retired to rest on the imperial couch between my regal comrades full of gratitude that I had discovered many things which were needful for the further progress of civilization.

CHAPTER XXX

HORROBOO RELIGION

We took the remaining sights of the town more leisurely. There was a circle where religion was kept but it was not to be seen. Griffelak related that the tribe, having been formerly harassed with it daily and finding it a wasteful exercise of the knees, brought it hither for deposit at high usury to be collected in the next world. Their theology, if not profound and poetical like ours, at least deserves the respect of civilization for its simplicity and ingenuity. 1. Man is finite in all but one attribute, they say, which is his weakness: he is infinitely weak. 2. The world is infinitely bad. 3. Infinite weakness cannot wrestle with infinite badness. 4. Only God, who is infinitely strong, can do so. 5. Therefore man may as well sit down and have a good time and let God wrestle. 6. The reward of sitting down and having a good time here will be heaven, for God is most honored by our recognizing his infinite power and letting him show it, and those who honor him in this way will receive the highest heavenly pay for their right attitude.

This religion by its natural strength had vanquished a number of rivals, wor the smiles of the state, and conquered for itself a high place in men's hearts, and it had been lodged on a platform elevated far up a vast perpendicular, capping four pillars composed of countless shaven trees spiced one above the other with thongs, commodiously situated in the enclosure; where, being placed as near the sky as could be reached in that climate and with their simple architecture, it did not conflict at all with the genuine affairs of life. Before the good time given by plank Five of their Religious Confession had extended much, it was voted by the nation that the principle of Division of Pleasure should be applied to it, as otherwise the world might not continue as bad as the perfect religion required it to be, when, after much urging, the fat consented to enjoy all the pleasure in order to deliver the rest from its gross earthly embarrassments.

It is generally believed by these pious Horroboos that men may become spirits while they live, in room of waiting to be so when they are dead; or if not invisible spirits at least visible ones, which is the religious vindication—or shall I rather say holy cause—of the Gourmands' depriving the community of nearly all nutriment. By starving the common people they bring them as near the blessed condition of beatified spirits as is attainable in this mundane stage of pain. Science and religion are diverted with this experiment, in which the semi-spirit people themselves even take some interest; it is the bridge of sighs whereon religion and science fraternize. A workingman without a body and capable of equal work with those in the flesh is the thing sought, to prove the immortality of the soul and reduce wages. He will need to eat nothing and can shovel with his spirit in lieu of arms.

CHAPTER XXXI.

The National Harem

Then there was the harem circle, almost oppressively
interesting on account of the exalted sentiment toward
women which forbade the recognition of their sex. There
were some foolish errors of nature difficult to reconcile
with the sublime spirituality of the Horroboo race, but
these errors were industriously ignored by the population
until the twenty-fifth year of each babe, after the wise
manner of civilized countries. Up till that time the national
system of education courageously affirmed the identity of
the sexes in everything. Before that age the erroneous
existence of sex was not mentioned to children. Prior to
that time, however, a system of instruction was allowed
in secret by a set of licensed teachers called Libertines,
who roved at large through society spreading vice and
disease, and it was generally believed that some progress
in understanding was made, tho this was never known for
the parents and grandparents and official teachers were
restrained by modesty from inquiring.

At twenty-five, while the heads of all were averted and
their brows were furrowed with terrible censure, the children were formally invited to make known what pseudo-
love diseases they had contracted up to that date, or what
injuries they had unwittingly done themselves on account
of the deathlike silence on these matters maintained by
all who were tenderly interested in their welfare. Following their disclosures the collected tribe sat down in the
gloomiest posture, as if they were in the lower exit of
purgatory, and all picked up handfuls of dirt and threw
them in the direction of the culprits, to symbolize the loathing in which such enormities were held and to ingrain the
solemnity of the warning. The emphasis of the occasion

was tremendous from the fact that all the elders had suffered in like manner from the same neglect. Then the
convocation arose and most of the men, taking their sons
by the hand, proceeded to the national seraglio.

For ample amends were made for these rigorous aus-
terities by the Grand Harem, a house of general corrup-
tion for the empire, for males of all ages from childhood
up. Fathers and sons met each other in this Temple of
Eros and exchanged confidential greetings and winks, with
jokes which all of them seemed very much to enjoy about
their wives, mothers, sisters and sweethearts. The girls
detailed to serve in the institution were chosen by lot*
and were given the choice between assuming this enlightened occupation and having their bodies sawed into two
parts under the heart. The choosers were about equally
divided in their affection for being sawn asunder and their
consecration to public duty, and the government signified
its displeasure toward those who elected the saw by placing
a tall foolscap on their heads as they were led along the
boulevards to the block.

The precious tribal modesty, which bloomed outside of
the harem like the tropical palm, was left at the gates of
this glorious circle, to be resumed when the visitors
emerged, and indeed so much modesty was daily consumed
on account of the vast amount of it exercised in education
and conversation, in the home and physiology classes, that
there was none left to be used in private anywhere.

There was one remarkable and unusual class of men
that kept entirely aloof from women, with a crabbed tem-
per of mind most inhuman toward the gentler sex. These

---

*I was compelled to acknowledge to His Highness that the Horroboo
method of selecting their prostitutes is eminently more fair and h·mane
than the Christian usage which grants a monopoly of this function
almost exclusively to the daughters of the laboring classes, and selfishly
endeavors to prohibit the young women of other ranks of society from
sharing its emoluments,

atrocious males, who were objects of rabid persecution from the rest of the tribe, also refused to be fathers of children, because they said the children could only make half-men so long as their mothers were but half-women. My own wrath was so intense toward these abhorrent creatures that I hit one of them a sharp cut with my stick as he passed us, to show him how civilization felt about it. The spotless married women replied to the slanderous action of these misogamists with the contemptuous silence it deserved, and spiced their contempt by remaining unintelligent and undeveloped with the sternest fortitude.

The respectable women philosophically recognized the Harem as one of the primal and necessary National institutions, equally divine with the family itself and the basis of its preservation, and made no outcry against it, blandly accepting the harem diseases which their husbands profusely brought home and imparted to them, as a destined dispensation of their diseased gods. This may startle you, as it did me until I came to understand the Horroboo philosophy on the subject. With the Horroboos every disease is sacred, and what is more wonderful every disease has its guardian deity, who is angry if a disease is cured. Their doctors are the priests of these gods and their function is to preserve the diseases from extinction. The longer they can keep a man sick, the more the grateful wretch pays them. It is also a part of their honored priestly code to protect the citizens from a knowledge of the laws of health, which not only pleases the diseased gods but deservedly enhances the revenues of the priestly doctors.

I was astounded at the information that every one of the gods who was the patron of a particular disease had that malady in a very aggravated form himself, and that naturally many of the doctors to each of these gods were likewise afflicted with the appropriate complaint. It was reasoned that without having a disease himself a doctor could not be perfectly competent to preserve it in another man's constitution. I noted them intently and could not deny that the physicians were faithfully devoted to their calling and pursued it so ably that no disease was ever allowed to become extinct, and for their devotion to the well-being of the diseases the appreciative people made many of them monstrously rich.

But especial credit was earned and received by those incomparable lights of medicine who were the protectors of harem diseases. Their success was so grand that nearly eighty per cent of the males of the empire were infected with these gay plagues at some time in their lives, only about twenty per cent of the population entirely missing their happy contamination. The indolent doctors who were responsible for this twenty per cent were bitingly censured by the rest of the medical fraternity and were drummed out of the profession for violation of the medical code. Of course the virtuous women benefitted indirectly by this excellent practice of the physicians, in having the harem maladies communicated to them and their children by their husbands at home, so that they did not miss the advantages of the harem plagues. These brilliant achievements of the diseases were due to a Horroboo medical law, re-enacted every year at the altars of the Horroboo Harem gods by the anointed harem physicians, that the existence of the harem diseases should always be solemnly denied by the doctors, with the most awful oaths to confirm the denial, and that the whole stunning array of jocund deaths resulting directly or indirectly from them should be publicly ascribed to inscrutable divine love with thanks to God for their infliction.

After mastering this Horroboo theology of disease, altho criticising it at some points by the blazing light of our superior Christian practice, I seemed to realize for the first time the divine economy of diseases and why we have them. The prolific idea of diseased gods dissipated the fogs.

CHAPTER XXXII

BUDDING ANGELS. THE BEAUTIFUL EMPRESS

"Here is a circle," quoth my royal guide, "which I vow is without parallel in the universe. It is the Pity Circle. Contiguous barbarians may outstrip us in the length of their feet and in some other marvels of the arts and sciences, but we claim pre-eminence in this. Here in this acre we sow the first idealets of the Infinite in the minds of our young, especially of our Gourmands' and our Sufferers' young. On Saturday afternoon once a month the most emaciated children are collected and brought hither to a matinee; they are placed in a shallow pit circumscribed by a rim on which the children of the Fat are pleasantly perched: the lean children are there to be pitied, the fat ones are there to pity them. We name the event our School of Social Pity. The true relation of classes is taught in this school. Here the fat youths learn to feel themselves infinite, and the lean learn to look up to them as so, and on themselves as infinitely finite; it is the first idea they all obtain of God. The fatlings furnish a collation of worms' feet and tears to the dear little shadows in the pit, the only meal of their skeleton guests during the month, owing to the stern decree of the Fat Fathers that the food surplus shall not be touched. The Fathers purpose to keep a pitiable class in tragically deep sorrow by the action of confirmed emptiness, in order to exercise their offspring in the qualities of pity and mercy, traits that would probably never appear in them at all if these most wretched objects of their attention did not exist.

"This excellent repast of worms' feet and tears is likewise another of those manifold agencies for saving the State, or the state of the Fat, by awakening early in the hungry spirits of the common sufferers a deep sense of gratitude for the favor shown by their superiors. Why, they would die if this banquet did not come monthly just when it does, and many of them die in spite of it!"

I professed regret that I could not witness one of these charitable ceremonies, so fraught with healing for broken hearts and abandoned digestions, when Griffelak joyfully exclaimed Whook! Whook! and drew a paper from the cowskin bag at his girdle and handed me the sheet: it was a copy of the Horroboo Public Defiler containing a graphic idyl of the last meeting of the Pity Society; I perused it and begged permission to keep the Defiler, which is now among my dearest souvenirs of Africa. It thus read:

"Horroboo Pity Day. Town ablaze with mercy. General downpour of pathetic tenderness. Union of the Four Hundred with the Forty Thousand, Full and Empty, with Kisses thrown down from above by the Full. A magnificent collection of bones unusually visible. Former displays surpassed. Roses and Rags. Unequal distribution of Fat. No Socialism at this dinner. Pity however equalizes happiness. Many tears gratefully received. Price of worms' feet forced up by the demand and the market skilfully cornered by the fat babies; they will be great speculators when they grow up. Beautiful ceremony of worship when the Emaciants fall on their knees to the Fatlings and promise them faithful service forever in return for Pity. Statue of Pity as a fat child erected in Obesity Park and the pitied swear allegiance to it. Their next meal one month from to-day. Life-preserving power of pity between meals. Prominent Digestions present at to-day's feast."

These were the headings in quite artistic Horrobesque type, followed by the calmer description:

" 'The givers of the feast were appropriately another 400 children of the well-to-do classes, who, as members of the Children's League of Pity—surely title was never more appropriate—are taking in early life an interest in the welfare of those who are less happily placed than themselves. The League of Pity is, of course, affiliated to the National Society, which has now a membership of nearly all the children of the Fat. Some of the darlings sturdily refuse to pity and prefer to stimulate the starving with pins. The 400 members who contributed to the cost of yesterday's entertainment included the children of the Duchess of Hooka-Porka, the Countess of Damnpeople, the Right-Hon. Lady Skintenant, the Hon. Lady Drinkblood, Lady Cramdaddle, Earl Heartripper, Lord Stealall'er and the Hon. A. Grabworker.

" 'While the guests were being entertained in the body of the King's Hall, the juvenile hosts and hostesses surveyed the fruit of their good work from the galleries, which were as well filled as the tables at which the feast was served.' One of the sweetest episodes occurred when 'the guests heartily responded to a call for cheers for the givers of the feast, Miss Toadwell (the secretary of the league), and the Empress, the patron of the society.' "

"Curious," said I, "London often has something like this too, and so far away from you! How could they have borrowed the idea?"

Griffelak bent his beetling brows upon me and said: "If our system of perfect equality ever fails, the union of all classes accomplished by these monthly spreads of pity is expected to cement the hearts of my countrymen to me and the fragments of state into a perduring conglomeration. If we can induce the fat to part with enough property to make a prize we shall offer one to the best pitier."

"Old Chap," I said banteringly, "you have been keeping some very delightful institutions in the background. There is Her Majesty, the Empress, your wife, mentioned by this paper, and the Nobility—where are they?"

"My Consort you shall see," responded his Ebony Highness, "but I beg you will not insist on looking into the

nobility. They are an experiment, just in the early graft.
Merely owning and eating all the food is getting to be an
old story and the Gluttons want new excitements and honors, as well as distinctions among themselves upon the
basis of their rank in flesh. We don't know yet how the
population will stand this. They are well contented with
the fact of their slavery and would never rebel against
that, but it is another thing to make a public memorandum
of it and to acknowledge the fact in a word: the institution
of nobility is all right so long as it isn't called so, but to
make it up into a phrase and inaugurate that phrase into
the language may cause a revolution. Humanity is an odd
snake, and you have to be careful of it. We are getting
psychologically ready by printing the idea daily in the
papers and ridiculing its danger or novelty; we suggestively
post the word 'nobility' on every public billboard to reclus-
ter the Horroboo affections, and time will root the institution in. But the Empress Queen shall be summoned."

Her Highness, whose dazzling beauty in the Horroboo
eye had been the cause of many court cabals and some
scandals not wholly favorable to the longevity of certain
highborn subjects, was brought forward in a sedan of
peeled sticks carried by six chained Ethiopians. She was
squat, swart and must pustulated, nevertheless with a distinguished bearing, no other indeed than six royal brothers,
the sons of a noble king who had been recently caught by
a great Horroboo commander with a brotherly letter under
a flag of truce, by being invited to dinner, and there while
drinking a bumper of amity beheaded from behind. In
case Griffelak should have no male issue it had been generally decided that this illustriously treacherous commander
should ascend the throne after him, to encourage the war
art of conquering difficult enemies by white flags, hospi-
talities and forgeries. I was sorry that I could not cable
these valuable ideas to some of our Philippine generals,
but there was unfortunately no cable.

Queen Griffelak-Stackwaddle-Wigwaggy took no interest in anything that I could see, further than to manifest a very picturesque contempt for the Emperor, and delight in the plaintive wails of a little Siamese poodle whose ears she returned to pulling viciously after her state introduction to me. Her most illustrious lineament was the noble construction of that part of her face where there is usually a nose. A wide forward-slanting plane obtained in that area, causing many envious Horroboo ladies of the peerage to amputate their own nasal extensions. I learned that she was famous throughout Africa as a leader of charity, for she sent a load of straw annually to the horses of the poor.

She was also devoted to art, being patroness of that famed Horroboo school of artists which has worked out the distinctive field of death agonies with so much glory. Her own gallery includes the brilliant collection of 5,000 pieces representing the Lean in every stage of death for 5,000 minutes before the final event, and as these are arranged in a line, the lover of art can, by slowly walking from one end to the other, gain a most vivid and pleasurable impression of the death-process, with the effect of our moving pictures except that in this case the spectator moves, whole by going in the other direction he obtains a beautiful realization of resurrection. The Empress herself dabbles a little in paints and is quite an adept in catching the changing expressions of starving infants. She has in fact received several prizes from the Horroboo Academy for her work, consisting of dead babies' eye-sockets—appropriately those of the very babies she had sketched best.

CHAPTER XXXIII

The Glories of Horroboo Science

After my many amazements in this wonderful country and feeling supersaturated with advanced light, I besought their highnesses to change the program of the fourth day, when it had been designed to conduct me through a circle of educational institutions presided over by the semicircular counsellors, on the plea that I could not remember half of the iridescent novelties I had already imbibed, tho secretly convinced that in matters of education they could not be one whit ahead of our universities, and not wishing to load myself with a repetition of civilized life, suggesting in place of a dismal day with the pedagogues a walk into the argent air of the campagna, for the smell of the war carcasses had become impregnably fortressed in the whole capital and I feared being made sick.

"We can accommodate you very well with the country and some education too, as this is the Field Day of the great Gluttonian University, our principal institution; the departments go out into the hills this morning to conduct their work."

This I thought would be something new. Each class took its station on a separate hillock and began affairs. The geologists were counting the grains of sand and commenced where they had ended on their last visit; they were to ascertain how many grains there were in Africa, and after that in the rest of the world. The botanists were counting the blades of grass. The meteorologists were counting the particles of fog in the air. The chemists and physicists were counting the atoms of the universe. The biologists were counting the hairs and cells of the animals. Psychologists were taking measured note of each other's snores, their multitude, their width, their cause, and the intervals between. Political economists were enumerating the bounties of the living Fat Men to their people, and historians were numbering the blessings past which had been publicly conferred by fat patriots now dead. There were students of language, beginning rightly with the grunt of Griffelak I. as the primary root of all language, and closely engaged in counting over the squeaks and sounds uttered by each man that had since lived, a task demanding a large and delicate ear and consummate erudition in all the sciences and languages, branches of mathematics and astronomy, higher classes being already devoted to sorting over and summing up the number, variety, key, circumstances of utterance, and motions of the aggregate of sounds that had emanated from the inhabitants of the stars. Advanced mathematics were subsidiary exercises to counting the latter and were consequently called higher. The obscurities to be untangled only made the results more fruitful when derived; for example, it had to be ascertained how many men had lived, before the sounds they had made could be counted, and the sounds of each individual then cast up separately. As fossils here came into play, the surface of the earth several miles deep as well as of the stars was to be dug over before the knowledge of languages could be called complete.

These original studies, or more properly original countings, were declared to be the components of a compendious total embracement of all being called philosophy, which they produced in this manner; human sounds are the expression of the soul of man, and other sounds (produced by nature) express the soul of the universe—therefore by collecting all the human sounds that have been uttered, and uniting them with those made by nature, a plenary comprehension of man's soul and of the infinite soul is secured. This is Philosophy. And thus moreover a practical guide of life will be obtained when all the countings are completely finished and added, being derived by working out the mathematical effect of every past act from the count, and deducing therefrom the effect of every proposed act before deciding to perform it. This is Ethics. I forgot to mention that the medical faculty was employed in counting the microbes of infinite being, which had suggested to a new sect of seekers after the soul to count the quantity of submicrobes domiciled in a microbe with the expectation of finding the pure and final soul element in the smallest of these.

I was enormously pleased that I had not gone away and missed their higher education in its broad-girthed ideality. "I am a university man," I said to Griffelak, "topped off with a seminary. My university was Scarvard, but I confess it falls a little short of yours in some points. Does this sound educational system of counting everything lead ultimately—I mean, of course, in the indefinite sometime, when every thing shall have been counted—to anyone's improvement? happiness? good? or to general social uplifting? or, er, such like?"

"To the fat men's," he answered, "it uplifts them. Education is composed of unfathomable mysteries. It is not yet but may sometime come to be the main pin on which society hangs, raised high by it above the turgid pool of self-contending chaos. It is with us a fast-anchored tradition that when all things here, hereafter and heretofore shall have been duly and accurately counted, as verified by a second count without deviation in any item from the first, the fat will be evicted, the food supply opened freely to all, the specter of famine banished, and happiness will return in a flood of undying light. To fend off this hideous apparition of looming joy is the problem of superior education, of universities, of semilunar instructors. The counsellors, or fat men's second selves, who manage the departments, collect a number of infinite tasks, many of them as impossible as they are useless, on whose completion (never to be) attention will be turned with the great (and useless) information derived, to the improvement of popular life, the removal of suffering, the good of mankind, the joy of the individual. With that ravishing goal in view all are stimulated to work ever and energetically on at counting, that labor of Sisyphus and Death, in perseverance wherein there is no escape for mankind from their chains to the Fat. As you may conjecture, the Fat have endowed this university richly and guard it jealously, spewing all thoughtful counters out of it gustily. Not only is counting an occupation not of the excellent parts of man's mind, but it is deadening to what is most excellent in him, reducing his finer perceptions to insensibility, so that he cannot see that his labors are carrying him away from the goal he thinks he is approaching. For nine thousand years, the age of the university, the tribe, particularly its young, have been counting faithfully; to this is due the progress and permanence of the venerated institutions you have reviewed, and they will be preserved by education until the world shall end its astral blusterings by some encounter with a wandering astronomical bully more monstrous." Thus spoke the ripple-tongued Horroboo, son of many scholars.

"And no counter ever sees the cheat and insanity of counting!" I sighed. "Mysterious!"

"Well, some do," he conceded. "The counting of the advanced students is called original work; the lower scholars learn by heart what these creative geniuses count. Once in a long while some advanced student says: 'We have now counted hard and enormously, let us employ the results of it as far as we have gone to the condition of our race and bring all the people up to the present level of our numbering.' 'Oh, no,' says the Counsellor, intoning, 'that would not do at all, for don't you know, our counting may yet be found to be wrong in some respect, so that if we began practical improvement now we should have to go back and undo it all by and by, and there would be a bitter disappointment and delay in reaching perfection. No, no, let us stand still and not wiggle or wink until the whole counting is done, and then jump straight over into the ineffable.' 'But,' says the student, still unconvinced, 'what is to recompense these generations of the past twelve thousand years and those of the twelve million years to come? Haven't they given their sorrow gratuitously? Can you pay one generation off by making another happy? Can you make it up to a needlessly miserable one by the hypothetical gayety of its posterity? With that bliss-bathed generation only to arrive twelve million years later? And when, after all, the most ultimate happiness of any is only a pacifying guess of yours?'

"Now, says the Counsellor, you land on the impregnable rock of theology as well as on the smaller stones of ethics, political economy and applied athletics. Theology rightly says we know nothing about this and should not ask; such knowledge belongs exclusively to God, and it is the highest godliness for us to live on the spikes of a guess; very likely God enjoys seeing his fellow creatures agonize, it appears so from looking at their history; and a race which cannot subsist on a mystery twelve million years is not fit to live and suffer. That is theology, and its last word is Die and Hope—die first and hope afterwards. Then comes ethics with some adhesiveness for those who didn't stick on the surface of theology. Says ethics, All this deadly human agony is for moral discipline, we discipline a few million generations for the good of those that follow; don't worry, you are being disciplined and that will be the end of you, but in twelve million years or so, when the disciplining and counting are done, some generations will come along and need no disciplining because the counting

is done—if a mistake in the numbers is not found, and then
it may be twenty-four million years, but what are a dozen
million years compared with accurate counting? So says
ethics, and catches several Horroboo students in its glue.
Now comes politcal economy and takes a shy at the still
unstuck. Says it: Natural law settles this, natural law
made man unequal intentionally, ergo it is only intended
that the Fat shall be happy; the rest of you miserable
beggars ought to be very much obliged to your Father
which is in Natural Law for begetting you at all and con-
ferring the curse of natural woe upon you. This catches
quite a number more, indeed all the hardheaded sound
reasoners, the alabaster wits and marble-brained geniuses
in a word, who all stick in a row behind the theological
and ethical rows. Then the department of applied athletics
arrives for the enlightenment of the remnant, and cracks
their heads in two with bludgeons and swords, and that
is the terminus of their skepticism. Thus by a reasonable
system of education are the spooks of intelligence expelled
from inquisitive childhood brains."

As I stood inscrutably meditating I was seized on either
side by my companions and hurried across a yawning gulch
up a perpendicular brow of brush-bearded nature to inter-
cept an approaching cavalcade in a path between two sen-
tinel rocks.

"How fortunate!" cried the Emperor gleefully, "I
had forgotten my orders to the Ministry to send out another
civilizing expedition to-day."

A band of African music walked with radiant tread in
front, on whose heels came four dervishes with a copy of
The All-Wisdom Book open upon an oblong platter of art-
fully latticed bolos; then a life-size image of the tribe's
Supreme Being, represented as dead;* then, mirabile! a

---

*It is, as I have before told you, the singular conceit of these nations
to emblemize all their gods as dead; they declared they felt much safer
with their deities in this condition, that since they had slaughtered
their Providences they had been much better waited upon.

corpulent monster and his wife! after them a pair of cir-
cumflex counsellors bearing tablets with the results of the
count of things up to that moment; and last, all clad in
priests' toggery, consisting of a skin bag six feet long by
eight inches in diameter flung across their shoulders and
from which as from a golf case I could see spears and
other affectionate implements of holiness protruding, tho
carefully screened from less observing eyes by a shroud of
gauze prayers, about seven thousand men whom nobody
would ever have mistaken to be anything but multimurder-
ers and who were in truth the convicts of the tribe, purposely bred by misuse and misery to their profession of
liberating souls from bodies, for militant ends. When not
piercing the bodies of the lost with their spears they perform the office of priest to the fallen and pierce their hearts
with the love of God. They all threw themselves on their
heads when they perceived the Emperor, except the fat
couple, who spit upon him, and the Emperor acknowledged
the salute by falling on his head to the pair of obese Carrion.

"Here is another spark of savagery striding forth to
burn lovingly in the blank void of heathendom," mumbled
the monarch, wiping away the blood which his ardent intimacy with the nettled rock had lured from his regnant
front, and ejecting some gravel from his eminent lips.

"Explain, Dread Monarch."

"We are undertaking to spread the light of Fatness over
the world; no people can be happy without its hundred
Gluttons; we cannot spare our hundred but we send out
two of them to some adjacent race which we wish to bless,
to found the institution and breed the remainder of it.
With the grace of heaven we shall soon lift all the nursery
peoples to our plane. We are obliged to contend against
many prejudices, but these are mostly contended against
by our priests, who convert themselves temporarily into

warriors, for which their previous profession of convict has finely qualified them, take their spears out of their sacred sacks, and chastise a number of the prejudiced natives with death; thereupon the fat proclaim their proprietorship of the converted nation's food and build an enclosure for its storage and decay. The Gluttons are great unifiers of the world; wherever they go my rule accompanies them; in time all the nations of Africa will be skipping joyfully into the spirit land under their reverend panoply."

CHAPTER XXXIV

We Stumble upon the Fountain of Happiness

As we sauntered townward we encountered a thousand men running in a circle about a personage sitting on springs under a palmleaf umbrella. The runners carried stone clubs and frequently struck at imaginary objects as they ran. At signals from the umbrella-man they reversed their course, dodged, jumped over, or darted between the legs of one another, fell upon all fours and ran like animals, skulked and crept on their bellies at a high rate of speed, curved themselves into a hoop about their clubs as an axle, connecting these with consummate skill into a long straight line, and trundled themselves forward with astonishing velocity, stretched themselves out on the ground in rows and rolled in parallel lines and zigzags, still parallel, and performed I cannot remember how many other strange maneuvers, most of them parallel.

The umbrella personage had scrambled out into the sun and given us his place, I waited for the Emperor to speak, he seemed disinclined and looked foolish, I finally had to start him.

"There is nothing to be ashamed of in a national game."

"It is the Domestic Guard," he admitted reluctantly.

"That *is* queer. I thought your perfect institutions preserved themselves—with the help of your educators."

"They do, but we have to have an institution for preserving the institutions." He spoke resentfully, as one caught thieving. "Perfect outward things cannot remove the depravity of the human heart. Neither perfection nor starvation can entirely quell irruptions."

"You keep the equilibrium of state by equality and a just balance of clubs, then; well, tell us about it, even Jove had thunderbolts and Jahweh military angels, all Christian civilization rests on the bomb-shell."

The silvery light of a smile glinted through his scowl and he began.

"All our hunters and carriers have to take their turn in the militia, we have a thousand in service at a time, who serve a month and are then replaced by another thousand. They suppress the insurrections of their fellow hunters and carriers and are loyal to Flesh and Throne as long as they are on guard duty; when they leave it they generally create an insurrection themselves, which is suppressed by the next monthly guard, composed of citizens who had been suppressed by the retiring regiment the previous term. So it goes in a constant rotation: the people who are rebelling to-day at the desperation of their lot, are put down by their companions who were rebelling for the same cause yesterday and will be doing so again tomorrow, when their military service expires. But the outbreak of tomorrow will be quelled by some of their friends and families who are rioting to-day, whose turn comes next to do the military work."

My power of surprise having long since died, I closed my mouth and turned my gaze upon the objects that were preparing themselves for usefulness by just then charging

one another in squads of fifty and laying on their clubs
where they could with something more than perfunctory
ceremony.   I leaned over and laid my hand on his knee:
"Griffelak, in the name of universal security tell me how
it is done."

He did so. "It is the effect of a word and a stained toenail. We stain the little toe-nails of the military blue and
green, excepting the officers, whose big toe-nails receive
the colors. It lasts just a month and then disappears suddenly. While they have on this magic stain they are vain,
haughty, overbearing and glad of the orders to kill others.
Yet we have found that their loyalty cannot be wholly
trusted without the assistance of some magic word: patri-
otically stimulated only by the toenail colors they are liable
to side with their fathers, sweethearts and brothers. The
mystic word is ool, tho alone it is too strong and has to
be diluted with other sounds; it has no meaning, but its
potency is like that of oxygen for life, but opposite. It
reduces all the faculties to a state of temporary death, except the faculty of hate and the desire to kill. As the Home
Guard rush against the members of their families and their
neighbors to quell an irruption, they shout the word in
mad ecstacy, feeling themselves fused into little suns of
bravery.

"At one time we gave them a piece of colored cloth to
carry between their lips suspended by a tooth, but this
was frequently lost or stolen. At the beginning of each
month I deliver to them the word and the stone clubs with
all the dreadful seriousness of my high office, deepened
by a piercing groan from the official groaners: sometimes
it is gool, sometimes mool, pool, rool, dool, fool, or in more
strenuous times when starvation is more suggestive than
usual we enlarge it, saying begool, bemool, berool, bedool,
befool, etc. Our reason for changing it is that loyalty to
a single expression wears out, the people seem to grow

tired of killing their friends from the same motive, and we have to invent a new sound to give them a new sanction for murder. Yet ool must ever be an ingredient or the witchery fails.

"Often in their struggle for freedom and food the people resist this fireside military, employing two modes of warfare—they endeavor to cut off the colored toenails of the soldiers to break the spell upon their minds, for this invariably follows if the nail is amputated or the color rubbed out; the militia are then abruptly able to see things as they are and to comprehend that they belong to the people whom they are slaughtering, in spite of stained toenails. But we circumvent this by putting a metal thimble over the toe, perforated so that the colors can be seen. Of late, however, the people have taken to amputating thimble, toe and all, while the militia are asleep, and we may be obliged to case the entire foot in metal. It will be a black day for peace and poverty if they ever get to lopping off both military legs.

"The other artifice of the people is the effort to deprive the soldiery of the power to utter the charmed ool word smoothly, by slitting their tongues, which sets them free from its mystery. To escape from this strange bondage to ool, the nation, with the exception of Me, the Gorgers, and the Counsellors, is conspiring to slit every tongue in the tribe and to remove the toenails of the children: it will make no difference if they do, we shall propose some new sound of loyalty to the Gluttons and Ourself, and no sooner will a thousand receive their appointment, badges and clubs, than they will lose their ordinary identity and fight for us until we give a new lot their turn. Thousands of counsellor philosophers having wasted their vitals seeking an explanation of this humano-bovine principle, killed many cattle in probing for it, and gone insane over its intricacies; the search is now interdicted for the preservation of the Horroboo brain."

"Destiny and all the mysteries surely fight for you and the hundred Gourmands," I said; "which proves design and Providence in things; they were intended to be just as they are, and as they are is best. God is in his world. At the same time all these common people of his and yours had better commit suicide and get out of it and leave it to Him and You."

Griffelak squirmed and answered vehemently: "Sire, Almighty One"—through the force of my personality he had at length succumbed to the conviction that I was the Supreme Being—"Sire, don't gird at a fellow King, you know the Gluttons and We are only secondary in this military affair, the Family Guard is for the protection of the people themselves, their homes, to protect each home from the other, and give them all peace through continual bloodshed. Without peace no man can starve in quiet. We recoil from disturbing the last days of sufferers.

"All the blessings of savagehood are contained in peace and order, which we find can be best inoculated into society by a daily administration of Domestic Serenity clubs. The most peaceful quality of our peace is the public bloodshed to preserve it. Just imagine the state of society if these food and freedom irruptions were not sternly trampled out! Not a fat man could eat in peace or drink in plenty! The wonderful system of food-rotting might be destroyed! Counting might be abolished! Dream-equality overthrown! Industry abrogated! For who would hunt game for the enclosures or carry the corpulent on their shoulders if the peaceful strokes of the military clubs languished? It is not for the Fat that we preserve order but for the people under the fat, that the fat may by thriving continue to bless them.

"I trust you now see that the Family Guard is not a bloodthirsty whim of anybody's."

On the fifth day Milto, incredibly improved in health, and I with a high relish for enlightened savage institutions, gathered our entourage together and returned home.

CHAPTER XXXV.

I Prepare to Depart, the Richest Man in the World. My Last Miracle

The days glided fleetly by, box after box of presents from Buzzrack was taken from the ground, gold was hourly added to gold; not long would it be before I should have as much as I could convey to the sea with all the pack beasts of the realm. The guides that had brought me were not due until the end of the year, a term I had no reason to await; altho but five months in Africa my dizzy yet well-earned success had made me the richest man in the world, the richest of all time, in sooth—provided I managed to regain civilization unrobbed. It was a risk to remain—who could tell what indecent thing might overtake me among these unbalanced mystics?

One thought tortured my reflections: I needed the assistance of fifty devoted menials for working my caravan through to the coast, to ward off the emotions of impetuous fanatics and to load and tend my cattle on the long journey, stiff work for a goodly company of able-bodied muleteers since the beasts would number about four thousand. I estimated that one man could manage and conduct eighty animals, so that fifty men would suffice for the whole outfit.

In other respects my plans had been long matured. The fortunate caravan which had been commissioned by heaven to supply my needs had brought along a great mass of leather-lined sacks and box material sawed into appropriate lengths and accompanied by nails, only needing to be hammered together. They must have expected favoritism from primitive stocks. From time to time I had put together a few score of these boxes as the gold heaps swelled, and when all of them, as well as the sacks, were filled I computed that it was as much as the four thousand beasts could be entrusted with, lest some should break down in the desert.

I will not say whether my pile of gold was so vast that some even then remained for me to bury in the nights, and which I revisited Africa to recover, or whether I buried and left it for a time not yet come of shocks and reverses in the business world, as a bank which cannot fail. I disrelish the excitement caused in white men by visions of buried treasure, even if it has since been dug up.

The selection of my camel drivers demanded keen judgment of men. I could trust neither the King nor the common sort for this trenchant service; the poor King was fast dwindling away, losing his last rays of mind, and could not live long, from no perceptible malady—which I could have cured with drugs,—but the great modern realities with which I had irrigated his soul had been more than he could physically absorb, I might say; they had crippled his vitals, the endeavor to fathom their purport had consumed his zest for life. It was a stroke from above from which I could not defend him. If one of the ordinary people should learn of my purposed exit with the shimmering dross he would too likely tattle as vulgar folks will and worship would change to nasty hate. In short, altho my warnings that the mineral was for another world had been peremptory, altho they understood that I was merely an instrument of Omnipotence, altho they had yielded to the laws of profit and right and given me a full quitclaim on gold and everything, I thought I could dimly sense a selfish distaste for my taking all this healthy capital out of their country; it gave them work where they formerly had none, it caused money to circulate freely, their salaries were liberal and prices high, so high that when they had paid the prices nothing was left of the salaries, for I, as the just owner of the productive agencies of the country, fixed and collected these prices before the salaries got out of sight. No wonder they did not wish their capital and capitalist to emigrate. They had never known prosperity before and if I went they would never know it again. No, the common people were not to be trusted.

There remained the great. Their morals were of a more liberal hue. They could be depended on to understand me, and cleave to civilization, and appreciate a good opening for themselves. They were free from the parochial bonds of loyalty which held the common mob together about their nation; they stood aloof from the patriotic drove in all things save acceptance of its feeding and favors, cordially despising it, boasting themselves to be of a different brand of blood, welcoming every occasion to do the gross crew that fed them harm. This was true not alone of those who had weltered in greatness for a few weeks but of all, tho they might have been reared to grandeur only twenty minutes before.

To fill out the necessary number, annulling civil service rules against my will, I therefore increased the great to fifty and invited them up to my cave one evening for a fellowship tea. It was an honor I had never before indulged them in and they came with fluttering trepidation.

"Leave your poles at the door, gentlemen," said I as they arrived, "let us waive ceremony among ourselves this evening and drink and chaffer as trusting financiers."

Then I took them into my confidence. "My friends," said I, "You are fitted by your graceful demeanor, shifty natural qualities and reptilian ambitions, to partake largely in the recuperation of the moral world now being conducted by the civilized; altho your skins are black your hearts are white, your souls have been schooled to the burden of great financial responsibilities, you would all of you make excellent capitalists and foreign travel would sit upon you lightly and become you well, I am inclined to consider you capable of drawing interest, you have bravely shown your ability to let other people work for you, your dispositions have been tried and found agreeably wanting in the qualities that make enlightened and fraternal men, your deportment toward inferiors is that of the tiger and boar in accordance with the ripest etiquet of civilization, you have a fine sense for getting what is not your own and making it appear that it is your own, as I saw at the inauguration ritual of the first vintage of rubies, you are fitted to play a larger part in the world than you can do cooped up among these short-sighted silurian hills. Here your diet is limited by the sparsity of the population, out in the great world there are more people than the leaves of the trees, most of them ready to be eaten if you approach them in the right way. Your associates here are beneath you: why vulgarly wear away your lives with the mean, when in other parts of the world there are nations on a par with you morally and inferior to you in the pigment of their skins? I will conduct you to these fragrant parts; we will load the camels, donkeys, mules and yourselves with gold and leave these wretched beings that surround us here, to cross the desert till we reach a paradise. What do you say to it?"

As when the skeptic orb of night peeps forth upon a Halloween, so peered I from the cynic azure of my skyful intellect upon a nameless antic. And when my crockery was all broken and even my bric-a-brac bemauled, they fretted to be gone that instant, only asking time to collect the beads of the multitude and clandestinely relieve the King of his portable possessions; I could depend on their silence they lustily vowed to the frighted night, and implicitly trust the sanctity of their oath to betray the tribe with fidelity.

My path was now clear. I secretly condensed my remaining goods for the excursion, leaving little to be done at the last. Then I notified the corporation that another box of glitter and dreams had arrived, more adorable than the others, and all accompanied me to the burial ground of the tenth jewel-case. It was filled with nickel watches, wind instruments of music for the innocent, dolls that could reason, glass eyes that could see, white neckties, hairpins, and every delirious object in which the savage and his bride delight; then came the miracle of the false bottom and the sweet things on which they now relied as a divine smile. The present confection excelled all others and was impregnated with a sure and deadly poison.

I was about to deliver my final stroke, as I had conceived it before enlisting in the missionary business at New York. It was necessary for this tribe, with whom I had lived on such singularly agreeable terms for almost half a year, to be exterminated in order that I might safely escape, and for this reason I had brought the sweets now to be administered. Could I have been assured of retiring in peace with my own, the heavens might have sunk into hades before I would have harmed a hair of their shaggy heads; indeed my affection had grown mightily intense for them, as I am sure had theirs for me; they were a guileless darling race of childlike beings—but there was the gold, my property, earned by a thousand risks and toils: to refuse me free passage with my own would be downright robbery, a corrupt assault on the property rights which I had established for their benefit, and I was justified in guarding against this potential outrage with pungent sagacity.

In distributing the candy equally as usual, the women and children getting their share, I slipped a harmless sort to the great men, who I intended should assign the destruction of their fellow countrymen to divine wrath. Commanding them to eat immediately I held my watch to time the result: in.twenty minutes the noble Rinyo tribe was no more.

I was really sorry to part with the faithful and pleasant creatures whom I had learned to love, who had spared my life on sundry tempting occasions and done me countless kindnesses, who cherished and revered me in the triple relation of father, god and proprietor, one above mortals, descended from the rainbows to be their guardian and advance their happiness, and who by hard labor which had ravaged the health of nine-tenths of them had made me the richest man within the fecund purity of astral light. I felt that I owed them something and would fain have rewarded them by sparing their lives if it could have been. It was a painful conflict of two duties: I must have enhazarded my wealth and jeopardized the unspeakable good to be done with it in civilization to a type of beings before whom these groveling cannibals were but pestiferous insects. Further reflection and earnest prayer convinced me that I really owed the ebony lobsters, which they practically were considering their morals, a very small debt if indeed any; viewed broadly and in the light of the Gospel, they still owed me something and I should have taken it had there been anything left. I had presented them with the Word, revealed political economy to their imperilled understandings, given them the holy sacrament of labor, laid the knightly rod of commerce and capitalism on their backs until their backs broke, taught them book-keeping to facilitate the reckoning of their debts to me, and held out other inducements for them to get on in the world and on to the tricks of the next, blessings for which gold could not pay nor love atone.

I had denied myself for them. For nearly six months I

had worked with them like a slave, confined to my seat in the shady observatory under the tree, and had enjoyed the pleasure of paying their board by not forbidding them the use of whatever their wives could find for them to eat on my estates, and during that time my salary had been limited to four billions in bullion with a few thousand millions in chance diamonds casually picked up. They ought to have been deeply thankful for their board and were less so than the occasion merited.

As to my life, it was neither their love nor leniency that had saved it, but my own Yankee skill; my instrinsic natural goodness had drawn their devotion out to me and they deserved no credit for this, the credit for my winsome sweetness being mine; my brain, the merit of which belonged to God above only, had extorted from their impious heathen labor-power the gold which burdened a soil otherwise useful for churches, real estate agents and rent. I mused with some enthusiasm on the benefit my gold would confer on civilization: it would preserve the normal value of money and deliver the creditor from the nature-appointed necessity of taking advantage of the debtor, to the hurt and horror of the former's good soul, for if gold should grow scarce and its value rise it would be the sainted economical duty of the creditor to require as much of it from his debtor as when the same was plentiful and cheap, to defend political economy from the contempt of the poor.

On the other hand, what could be more base and useless than these sodden atrocities called creatures, mistakenly wearing the shape of men, whose highest notion of happiness was devouring one another, whose principal theory of usefulness was licking one another's feet, who envied and despised each other by a dogma no less empty and atheistical than the length of certain wooden sticks borne distressingly upon their iliums, impeding every healthy and pleasur-

able activity, whose women had no higher conception of
the loftiness of human womanhood than to meanly exist
knitting leaves together by ridiculous rules to maintain an
artificial standard for mutual contempt and hate?　Such
people were a layer of slag upon the anxiously pregnant
earth, hideous, anomalous, choking down the useful and
beautiful verdure of sprouting syndicates,—he who should
have the courage and power to remove them would deserve blessings from the human race, Rinyos of course
excepted.

It had really become a duty, too, their compassionate
extermination, as in mercy we mitigate the sorrows of sick
animals by death.　Labor had hopelessly sucked out their
racial stamina, even the women and children were paling
shadows since I had finally sent them into the diggings to
lessen the cost of production and break up their unholy
idling over fashions, needles and leaves.　They could not
adapt themselves and perished in shoals.　After that edict
board became more scrappy and unfeeding.　It was their
own fault, they would continue weaving their leaves, and
since they could not do so by day they sat up all night,
which I considered an outrageous disregard of health, and
was compelled by it to withdraw my sympathy. The sweet-
natured King had been nearing his death-bed for weeks
and a few more brief fortnights would have parted us forever (for he was not converted), through the sad ordinary
course of fading nature; I should only have deferred my
grief for the separation by waiting, and I loved to have sad
scenes pass.

So, as I looked upon the thousands of corpses of my former intimates lying stark athwart the mesa with set agon-
ized faces, a great joy filled my soul for what I had done,
strength coursed through my veins in the vision of further
usefulness before me, and I called the great men to my
side to witness that a sternly benevolent Avenger had

struck their nation dead for its filthy sins, only sparing them because of their pearly cosmopolitan virtues.

CHAPTER XXXVI

THE SIGN OF THE NOSE

My work was done and on the second morning after the sacrifice a noble caravan moved out of the now desolate valley of the tribe of Rinyo. I prepared the guns of the recently extinct prospectors for use, having had a dream that my life was sometime to be saved by firearms. Some delays occurred on the march owing to the obstinate resolution of the great men to wear their poles as they walked. In vain I expostulated, in vain I dilated upon their present strenuous equality, emancipating them from the irksome need to wear insignia of height, since, all their inferiors being luckily dead, they were disagreeably superior to none. This was the direfulest blunder of my checkered African holiday.

"If none are inferior to us, tell us the gain of being superior," they subtly wept. "What profits it us to be superior persons unless we are superior to somebody? Why, Holiness, you can't be superior in that case, you become just a common mean individual on the lowest level, nobody looks up to you, nobody's servility reminds you of your grandeur and goodness, there are no props or buoys or wings to your higher aspirations,—we prefer death."

They were profoundly grieved, listless, dispirited, their apathy deprived them of appetite and strength; if it were permitted to great men to have friends, the loss of all theirs could not have stricken them worse.

I sought to cheer them. "You are as great as ever," said I; "it hasn't affected your quality nor diminished your intrinsic selves that those below you are no more."

"It has destroyed our station in life," they cried, the banks of their eyes again swept with raging tears, "it has taken away those whom we despised and hated to see alive, now we can despise no longer, you have stolen away our joy."

"Well, well; don't cry, don't be unhappy, it will pass off, you will forget it; put on your poles and let us wag along or you will never reach paradise."

They did so, sobbing sorely, but they would eat no breakfast. I mounted the camel that bore a sack of revolvers, expecting trouble before sunset and keeping in the rear of the line to observe transactions, also leading a mule padded with rifles and shot guns. The natives muttered and chattered together with increasing vehemence, gesticulating like politicians about to nominate a president. At ten o'clock they collected their animals in a group and leaving them with two or three guards came plunging toward me clanking their poles, brandishing their spears, and would you believe it? swearing full-bearded American oaths. I have owed my life to many odd things in its course but never to anything so ridiculous as these savage escutcheon poles which they would not even now lay off for fear of curdling their haughty cream blood. It gave me time to unlimber my long-toms and retire behind the rampart of my kneeling camel. A rifle served at far range and I stretched a brace of the foremost aristocrats on the plain; then followed a broadside of buckshot which perforated some and struck all panicky and brought on a premature discharge of their shafts, too soon to do me harm. Not wishing to more than decimate them, from the value of mule drivers to my cause, I leaped the barrier and made at them with a shotgun in either hand and revolvers numerously dispersed over my person. A shot or two into the air finished the business, they fled precipitately, nor would they stop until nearly out of sight, certain that my machines would carry death as far as the eye could reach.

The guards of the beasts were utterly craven, but it was hours before I could entice the others back, who sat on knolls like prairie-dogs, staring and smelling disconsolately at the camp where I had prepared a savory meal of their dead companions, numbering four, as bait. Hunger overcame them at length; one by one they stole in, but before allowing them to eat I had each thoroughly flogged by his comrades. Altho it was near evening I compelled them forward through the sand, bearing their poles on their bleeding hips, until they could not move another step, when we pitched our camp for what remained of the night.

I imagined they would be grateful for sleep after a day of such liveliness, tho naturally I was not, but what did several of them do when silence reigned but stealthily arise and run themselves through with their own pikes, moaning distractedly in their last breath that life was not to be lived if they could not be more virtuous than others. From time to time through the ghostly hours some one arose and shortened the pole of his nearest comrade and returned to rest with a transfigured smile of heavenly repose. I know not what the effect of these perfidious acts would have been on the victims if it had not appeared when the morning porter took down the shutters of heaven that each survivor had so shortened his neighbor's pole to curtail his honor that all were still equal. The expressive countenances of these ferocious extortioners when the discovery was made would have formed the germ of a new school of art.

On the morrow the day and the caravan dragged drearily forward while I pondered what should be done. It was clear that the pitiful drooping wretches could not long survive, bereft of their motive to breathe; when night came they sank upon the sands and slept tearless and foodless: then I undid their poles with great caution and made a bonfire of them. On their awaking I called them to me

and delivered the quickening information that we were to
have a restoration of inferiority.

"In place of the poles you will now have the Order of
the Cord. You have all shown a parallel proficiency in
licking, so that the poles are no longer marks of excep-
tional greatness, but I shall be very much astounded if
we do not find something in which all are not on a par.
If not, nature is no longer just and squint-eyed. We will
determine who is the greatest man by his bravery."

They capered gleefully at this news and asked how they
were to decide the tournament, jumping up and down
unpleasantly close on every side of me. "Shall we fight one
another and adjudge the conquerors to be the bravest in
the order of the number of foes that they overcome?"
And I thought they would begin to beat each other to death
then and there.

"No, no!" thundered I authoritatively, shooting two
revolvers into the ground for emphasis. "Don't you see
how wasteful of human misery that would be, destroying
some who might just as well live to be despised, and contracting the victors' area of happiness and contempt by
putting some of the possible objects of their scorn out of
the world? How frivolous! When will you learn to think
before you act! And can't you understand that this would
be no test of bravery either? For the beaten ones might
possess as much courage as the others, but their strength
might give out or an untimely blow lay them senseless or
dead. Fighting is merely a measure of brute strength, skill
or luck, but not the least of bravery."

"How can we decide, Lord God?" they asked, baffled.
"If bravery is such an inward matter who is to weigh
it?"

"Think," urged I, as they stood about me like school-
boys, with blankly open mouths. It was no use, they had
no heredity behind them.

"Use the Socratic method," said I, "there's money in it,"—looking affectionately at my saddled gold. "The bravest man may often be beaten, may he not?"

"He may."

"Because his strength is gone?"

"Quite so."

"But his courage may still remain?"

"Certainly."

"And if he had strength would he still continue the fight?"

"Most assuredly he would."

"How then is he to show that although his strength is gone his courage remains?"

"That is no simple matter, O Colonel Brady, the argument grows complicated; tell us how if you know."

"Is it not by manfully continuing to endure the beating which he has not strength to repel, not wailing or complaining, but with an exultant heart and joyous smile inviting the blows and earnestly petitioning his foe never to cease striking while he is alive?"

"That would indeed seem to be the mark of the perfect and consummate hero."

"And that," I said, "is the method we will now pursue. The cheeks are a part of the body with little if any importance to the economy of the whole but to keep in food for a transitory period until deglutition supervenes: is that so?"

"It is," they said, "since you assert it, and magically your words glide."

"Moreover, they are a positive hindrance to the functions of nature, enabling only a small quantity of food to be taken into the mouth at a time, drowning and smothering the voice, which otherwise might go out on all sides of the face at once, preventing us from learning to talk to different persons with the two sides of our tongue at the same time, and keeping the teeth buried away in the dark from the healthy microbe-killing action of the sun."

"It is reasonable," they assented, "and modern."

"Still, I have not mentioned all the disadvantages of the cheeks. The resources which nature builds into them might be applied elsewhere to the construction of useful muscle or even brain, without them men could not grow unsightly hairs over their countenances to falsify their true lineaments, the cheeks conceal the thoughts of the mind and therefore make us liars, acting as a mask or second screen before the brain, as is proven by the superior expressiveness of a naked skull, but most of all they prevent the entire tongue from being used in licking, with no impediment, on a grand scale."

My last hit appealed to their everyday perceptions and they cheered.

"To discover your greatness and bravery and to free you from these invidious appendages, I shall have your cheeks cut away little by little from day to day, and those who endure the pain with the slightest outward evidences will be pronounced the bravest and greatest among you."

"But how will it be known and remembered which is greatest if we have on no poles to display it?"

"By the Order of the Cord, and the Sign of the Nose. All of you shall wear a rope around your waists trailing out behind, the greatest being honored by dragging after him the mightiest attachment. But of the rest later, let us get to work with the knives for the time is passing."

When the first operation was over the caravan moved forward suffering pitifully but nobly stoical and with all signs of discontent gone. They must have credit for scoring magnificent fortitude. Several times a day the surgery was repeated, each one making a wider gap in their cheeks, but they certified true greatness of soul by steadfast silence and placid immobility of remaining features. You may not

believe it, yet I positively assert that having cut away all
their cheeks in vain, I was obliged to spread on a blister
of pepper and salt brightened with tabasco sauce before
I could distinguish the variations of their endurance. Their
health through this ordeal was wonderful, sustained un-
doubtedly by the keen anticipations of pleasure and quality
to come, when the contest should be decided. The salt
nevertheless brought them down one by one so that on the
fifth day came the distribution of honors. First, I conferred on each of them a codfish tail of equal size in permanent reminder of their human identity, fearing they
might drift apart into separate species; then their cords,
a number of clotheslines taken from the vanquished caravan, which they were conveying into the wilderness for
domestic purposes after marriage with the natives. These
being cut into appropriate lengths, one about ninety feet
long was connected with the greatest man. It did my soul
good to see him parade up and down the sand, ever glanc-
ing vainly back at the feather which he had tied to the
rope's far end the more distinctly to recognize his magnificence.

Through a luckless miscalculation of mine the rope gave
out before going around, and to correct the deficiency I
proposed a moderate general shortening, only to meet a
downright refusal from those in possession, who would
give up nothing. Fortunately there was a spool of barbed
wire in the outfit. I know not for what purpose the gold
hunters had brought it unless to protect their claims from
one another, but it was a godsend to me: unrolling several
coils while all the fashionable society fluttered about looking on, I was going to snip off a few feet for the inferior-
most when the others, who already had ropes, gave vent
to a new cry of indignant opposition. The upshot of it
was, they regarded the barbed wire as a higher distinction
than the rope, wherefore to pacify them I was obliged to

begin all over again, meting out ninety feet of barbed wire to the greatest—for he would accept no less—and proportionate quantities to the others as long as the wire lasted. The case was now almost as bad as when they had the poles, for they were constantly lacerating themselves with the wire, frightening the camels, and getting caught in the stones and bushes as they strained along. But I was growing tired of resistance and concluded to bear my trials like a Christian as long as food held out.

They did not forget my promise to endow them with other proofs of superiority and they were soon clamoring for the Sign of the Nose. I made them an oration explaining the nature of these signs and declaring that I should not insist upon their adoption; but as they were obstreperous in the affirmative I reluctantly set about their gratification. There were forty-two survivors, and I specified that the lowest fifteen must be contented with their cords until some above them died. Of the sixteenth from the bottom I cut off one toe, of the seventeenth two, and so went on advancing them in greatness until the thirty-fifth was reached, whose superiority to those before him was shown by the amputation of his twenty fingers and toes. There remained the greatest seven. First I removed the fingers and toes of them all that they might not be in any attribute less than the preceding; of number thirty-six I took off an ear, of the next both ears, then both ears and had the hair pulled out of one side of the head, of the next in order the hair on both sides, then all this and the extinguishment of one eye, number forty-one parted with both eyes, and finally the chief man received all these marks of greatness and the supreme one, the amputation of his nose, because it was called the Sign of the Nose. The last two being sightless could do nothing, but of the very greatest it is usual to expect little.

I anticipated some of the martyrs to die of their mutilations but happily none did. Their blood was gushing fast and of good quality from living overnight with jubilant images of once more dealing and receiving the blows of affliction, so they were somewhat recovered from the shattering months of gold digging and their flesh quickly basted itself together. Each fortified himself for the hardships of the days to come by hoping for the death of some one over him in rank, when he would be promoted toward the top by the loss of a finger, his hair, an eye, or a nose.

CHAPTER XXXVII

MILLIONS OF MAD CANNIBALS. THE HAND OF PROVIDENCE

And there were, I am sorry to say, hardships. We lost our way and were attacked by the bloodthirsty two-legged man-eaters into whose jungles we had inadvertently wandered, and not having time to convert them to their own destruction it was necessary to forcibly stand them off. Hordes of their fiercest demons came sweeping rudely in upon us from every side, thoughtlessly bent on our instant annihilation; my feeble few were crippled so that a third of them could not draw a bow; and yet we were saved by one of those miracles which always attended my course and which to this day I look upon as divine interpositions, probably secured by my missionary standing. As the dense black races approached, for many had joined to stamp us out, whooping and lashing themselves into a very lustiness of courage and anger, upon the foremost ranks broke the ghastly spectacle of my warriors' cheekless visages, the horrible red scars forming huge terrifying apertures from ear to ear and eye to lower maxillary bone, with the gums and teeth protruding fearfully, some also eyeless, earless, hairless or noseless, and they mistook this

smart set for devils just out of hell as they looked. Panic
seized their marrow. Turning they plunged back maniacally
into the shrieking mass behind, who had not yet observed
the fiendish expression of my company and still pressed
madly forward, imagining they were attacked. They fell
on one another and fought like scalded tigers; those who
saw the faces of my men being possessed by a cruel fear,
murderously attempted to tear their way through the
oncoming black wall: and while we sat calmly, never
lifting a hand or offering resistance—for there was nothing
to resist—and I lighted my pipe, these men tore one another to death, the rear host believing they were fighting
us made manifold by some black art, until thousands of
dead strewed the soft green sward and the relics fled.

My religious emotions had been somewhat inactive on
account of my infidel environment up to the present time
but they now blossomed forth irrepressibly. I taught my
wild guard to sing te deums to their Savior for our splendid
deliverance, pointing to the bloody field as evidence of
divine protection and love, which was so unmistakable
that even these dwarfed, gnarled and scrubby intellects
absorbed the lesson. I succeeded in converting nearly
half of them to Christianity, which cleansed my conscience
of a cloudy feeling that I had not done my whole duty
by the missionary society that sent me out, an omission
I had intended to make good by a decent yellow contribution. As this obligation was now liquidated the gold
could be applied to a university bearing my name which
I had in contemplation, the Colonel Fessenden Brady University, of Boston, where it would have a great field to
shine in by itself with no palpable competitor, with a department or two devoted to civilizing wasted savages in
Asia, Boston and Africa, and several departments on the
commercial attributes of God, with an eye to the amusing
traces of some derelict and rudimentary moral organs of

His, extinct in the solar system since the death of the ancient Greeks, and I sat up that night writing a letter to inform the Missionary Society of the number of souls I had saved and the perilous situations that I had been obliged to occupy in order to save them.

While I sat recalling my native language and meditating the appropriate religious terminology, imprecations arose in the direction of the largest mound of slain. Fearing new enemies and realizing that they could not see my people in the dark, whose countenances, or deficiency of countenances, were our sole protection, I hastily lighted a mass of fuel beforehand provided, calling upon my men to rise and expose themselves. Not one of them was in camp—but neither was there an enemy near. The din was caused by a hot altercation in progress between two groups of them. Rushing between hostilities in time to avert violence, what should I find but that my converts from heathendom had risen in the stillness of the infinite night and gone out to lay claim to all the corpses in the field; the others, also watchful, had followed them, and beginning with scholarly theological argument they were far on the road to religious persecution and bloodletting.

"What is this all about?" I demanded angrily, out of all patience. The new Christians answered volubly.

"The great God you told us of who now belongs to us, the one that slew all these vermin enemies for our good, surely didn't do it for these unsaved pagans in our midst who do not believe in Him—it was for us, his disciples. Now with lowly befitting humility, for God's will be done, Hallelujah! we declare that we have no vital animosity toward these evil wretches who refuse to be converted, if they keep their hands off God's bounties and control their greed,—and thus we prove our Christian spirit; for in their unregenerate vileness they are no better than the foreign devils whom our loving God slew, and we wonder at him for not slaying them also."

I expostulated, I reasoned, I pleaded. "You fools you!" I finally blurted out, boiling, "Can't you see that there are five hundred times more corpses than all of you can eat? We shall have to go on and leave most of them to rot anyhow."

But the converts sat like the lockjaw and declared that it was their religious duty to the good Sky-Owner to keep the whole. As for themselves they disclaimed all personal interest in the corpses, affirming that they were only performing a hard and selfdenying service to the Supreme. They called their brethren unconverted savages and imagined themselves as having covered many centuries of progress during the preceding night, in fact catching up the word 'civilized' which they had sometimes heard me utter, and christening themselves with it:

"Do not ask civilized Christians, who are assured of immortality and already feel pardoning bliss in their bones, to dwell with polluted heathen who have rejected the free gift of divine grace, whose morals are execrable, whose education is limited to stealing by brute force, and who have never learned that it is the greatest sin against heaven for the surface of the body, which heaven made with its eyes shut, to be seen. Look at their pagan nakedness!" This was the absurd manner of their talk, and they argued so keenly that I felt they had taken the very words I should have used under similar circumstances out of my mouth and I hated them.

How was I to deal with such stubborn donkeys? After sitting there an hour in the dark and cold, for the fire had gone out, it came to me to propose a solution. I thus addressed them: "If our God means you to have all these rich cadavers he will reveal it to you by enabling you to eat them all. Go at them now and eat up every one of these dead things, and know that if you do not succeed it is because your Jehovah intends the others to have some too"—so they began to devour.

They ate for their stomachs' sake until they were full, and then continued on for their religion's sake the rest of the night, while the other savages looked on dubiously with crucified desires, believing that the new religion would enable their adversaries to swallow everything there was, and therefore wavering and nearly ready to be converted to this all-absorbing faith. It was also a trying time for me, for I feared that the spirit of progress would again exercise the Christians if they failed, and cause them to discover a new motive for abolishing the heathen in their iniquity, which would force me to abandon part of my gold. Except for this I should have been in full sympathy with them. In principle they were right. They had comprehended and embraced the divine conception toward the world, they had adopted the principles of civilization, or intended to do so as soon as they could purchase the necessary clothes-stuffs, and it was plain that they appreciated the spirit of civilization perfectly and were already permeated by its ennobling sentiments. Hence I was naturally on their side. I owed it to my religion to be so. Still, I could not sacrifice money, even for the advantage of turning darkness into light by putting out the light of a few dark countenances.

I little knew the savage capacity. They ate until they were gorged, then they ate on till they were unconscious, and even then their jaws continued to move digestively. Only three or four died of this gluttony. Forty-six hours later the survivors came to themselves ready to acknowledge that it was not the purpose of the supreme god for them to have everything on that occasion, lifting the dark menace of Christian consecration from my mind. As long as they stayed with me however, I was unable to dislodge the idea from their heads that having everything was a Christian privilege and function.

On our march we met with strange phenomena. The

savage villages in our pathway were deserted, while in each we found meals of freshly sacrified human flesh, in every instance upon the choicest family plate. It was fortunate that I had early learned to enjoy the staple article of international diet, for otherwise I should have fared sorrily in these wilds, the non-human articles of food being very thin and singular. What was the meaning of the terror and worship we inspired everywhere in advance? I told my companions that gods and civilization universally had this effect upon the unconverted, but in my heart I knew well it was because we were taken for devils.

God or devil, my purpose was served just the same. After nearly three weeks of trials and wandering we reached the summit of a mountain pass and there below us a day's journey only, over a country whose character with its welcome adorning evidences of the white man's presence, was strikingly different from the barbaric rawness in our rear, lay the ocean and a military harbor town.

I needed my great men no longer; how should I disencumber myself of their richly emetic presences? Their surprisingly frightful appearance would involve me in trouble with the whites, while if we chanced upon inlanders with whom to converse they would be slyly boastful over the righteous fate of their tribe; or some of those unprincipled adventurers in which every African port abounds would be worming after information of the contents of my packs. I could not elude them nor could I turn them loose like cattle, for they would not go, and a scandalous shame it would have been to leave them trespassing about the veldt, carrying consternation among the innocent as so many loose satans, until they were ignominiously exterminated, which was sure to eventually and painfully happen. Human life is to me precious and sacred, and I think we are warranted in holding our own to be the most sacred part of it. I resolved to appoint Fate the arbiter.

"Come, boys," I said, "paradise is near and tonight you shall celebrate." From one of the bales I undid a keg of precious spirits, and from another some long bladed daggers which I distributed, saying, "You may have to fight your way into paradise, people often do in the present uncertain state of theology." Those bereft of fingers were at a disadvantage in handling these weapons but they could wield them with the stubs of their hands joined.

Rum was a new sensation to these fallow creatures, so were evangelical dirks—what more need I say? A fervent night of bacchanalian symphony is better than a long and tedious life vacant of rapturous thrills and spirit puissances. Black men have much to die for in this life and but little to live for. As to the sinners of my flock, they were a menace to mankind and I was glad to have them called down.

In the morning I pressed on alone to the town, where I found a British troop in possession and a vessel soon to depart for London, in which I took passage. Not to arouse the cupidity of the ship's people I spoke lightly of the value of my merchandise, too lightly, for a fearful storm overtook us and before I knew what was going on they had heaved half of my precious storage into the morgue of the sea. I cursed the hour of my birth but concluded to save the rest by taking the captain into my confidence, for I was still a thirty-fold Croesus with enough to command the preliminaries of American repose, who extorted a heavy indemnity for sparing me and not pooling the whole of my African traffic in his private person. In truth, this excessive scoundrel declared that he would have me thrown overboard and possess himself of what remained of my enormous happiness if I did not share it equally with him. Not feeling myself bound by a promise wickedly extracted through force, on reaching England I turned the lewd fellow over to the leisures of the law, where in due time he received a proper sentence for his illiterate ethics, and my own was restored. Although half of my original treasure and heart were gone I was still hugely rich with the preserved moiety, and when it was safely lodged in the Bank of England I felt that the primary purposes of human life had been achieved."

Colonel Brady paused, swallowed another glass of champagne, as he had done from time to time during his narrative, and concluded by saying:

Gentlemen, I have told you a long and surprising story, now for the first time issued from the press of my lips, but I swear to you that every word is true.

CHAPTER XXXVIII

The African Prince

For some time after the history, listened to with breathless tension by us all, was concluded, no word was spoken. Brady continued to drink, and with strained feelings we rose by common consent and filed unsteadily to the deck, leaving him tippling. The mighty hand-formed monster of the deep was plunging on through the strident swells of the insolent sea, the wind pounded and cut our faces and whistled with savage deviltry through the spars, it was a huge and realistic entertainment for the beginning of a year, ruggedly suggestive of inappeasable civilization and progress.

Some of us talked together a few minutes, most speakers warmly lauding the Colonel as an able, amazing, far-planning man of the world, one of its stirling ornaments; as for me I was choked with loathing for the villain, and two or three others shared my horror. We who felt thus drew together and remained a while in the booming blizzard to lull the tempest of our nerves. As we stood in the shadow Colonel Brady issued forth, staggering tipsy, and shambled slowly away from us; the tall dark young man who had listened to the story sauntered by his side supporting him. In a dim place where we could barely see their forms they stopped and seemed to converse; then, before we could realize, or act, or cry out, we saw the giant lift Brady clean into the air above his head, hold him there squirming a second, and hurl him far over the rail into the boiling flood.

We ran forward along the rocking deck and sprang upon the murderer as he stood calmly supporting himself by a stanchion and pensively contemplating the surge; he did not resist, though his leonine strength against three sedentary men of the street must have caused a momentary inconvenience to us.

"Gentlemen," he said, in broken English but with nobly commanding dignity, "I am at your mercy, one man cannot cope with so many, I have no desire for your lives, do with me as you will: I now care not what becomes of me, the sole object of my bitter existence is accomplished."

"What do you mean?" we demanded, nonplussed.

"I am the Prince of the African tribe which that reptile destroyed, the only son of the trusting King whom he betrayed."

We did not give the alarm. On such a night nothing could have saved the wretched life floundering in its ruin, and besides, the feeling hot and uppermost in every one of us then was how richly the infamous Brady deserved his tardy doom.

The Prince delivered his story with a truthful simplicity and a passionate intensity of feeling which none of us could distrust. While the missionary was conducting his

nefarious intrigue he had been absent from home on a
far expedition winning by adventure the qualities to reign,
a Rinyo custom answering he understood to the education
of heirs apparent in European nations to prepare them for
thrones. When he returned the stays of life were broken.
During the twenty moons of faithful mountain climbing
to fit him for the lofty duties of state, he had fallen in with
some civilized white-skins from Berlin and Chicago, who
had furnished him with a small knowledge of English and
German, a large knowledge of gold and its natural right,
as the best of earthly things, to survive over man, and
some notion of the white-man's native frolics beyond the
wave, in return accepting his various accoutrements and
traveling companions and allowing him to contribute his
services as a pack-bearer, until through the illegal agency
of an earthquake he had escaped.

When his sorrowful eyes fell upon the whitened vestiges
of his departed kindred he perceived that the first blessings
of civilization had arrived, and there on his stricken knees
pledged himself to devote his whole life to revenge. At
first it was his mad resolve to travel through the civilized
world killing whomsoever he could, trusting to Providence
to preserve him in this sacred work through many useful
years. In poignant agony he had tarried to wrest from
his ancestral parks a mass of the all-conquering sun-colored
weapon of enlightenment, and as he was starting vaguely
forth in quest of some clue to the murderers, or of whites
on whom to expend the first spasms of his vengeance, one
of his own people had wandered in, wearing hardly the
similitude of human expression, all his features save one
eye and his nose being gone, while, most wonderful to
relate. he was possessed of the mania for cutting off even
his nose to further enhance his consequence. This distress-
ful ghost had divulged all the cruel past, meantime implor-
ing the Prince to cut away his own fingers, ears and nose,

and to destroy his eyes that he might become, as the son of a King deserved to be, the greatest being alive.

The Prince had immediately sailed for Europe, where presently he saw that his quest would be favorably promoted by less prominence of his royal African culture and some training in surrounding usages, and he had submitted to rigorous private polishings to scour off the outer manifestations of savagery, so far as he could endure them, at the hands of the best masters. Then, accompanied by several Oxford Fellows whom he took into his pay as friends, keeping them ignorant of the object of his devious courses, he had drifted through the great cities of the old and new worlds seeking his foe. But he had failed, for this astute financier had shrewdly buried his identity in trackless oblivion, if he had not through the wrath of astonished heaven or his own alarmed repentance vanished from the remorseful flesh. Had he not perchance been perpetually mocked and scourged by the apparition of his impending fate? And yet, the strange confluence of the two on this ocean ship and the unsearchable accident of this New Year's tale were all that had finally revealed him. It was well, for having followed the phantom trail without a gleam of light through ten years, the Prince's faith in the dogma of eternal justice was fading; now, having strangled the career of this arch transgressor, his repose in the abiding verities was restored, he again loved God and was prepared to meet his Maker with ardent cordiality and calm.

Such was the confession of the poor Prince whose nation had been wiped out by the abandoned infamy of him whose breathless body now floated far in our wake. Returning to the smoking-room with the Prince, for whom we discovered something of the veneration always appropriately stirred by royal presences in the sensitive hearts of our foremost countrymen, with a due degree of pride in the exalted acquaintanceship, we consulted together beyond His Highness' bereaved hearing what was incumbent on us to do. We found ourselves spontaneously of one mind: the Prince had done his duty, the wretched Brady was where he belonged, and we would keep our tongues in our teeth about what we had seen. In the morning, when the Colonel's disappearance should become noised, the others of our smoking-room set would relate that he was last seen drinking himself drunk, and all the ship would conclude that he had gone out later and rolled overboard. We communicated our decision to the Prince and pledged abiding secrecy, warmly shaking him by the hand, which deeply affected his impulsive primitive nature. At his suggestion we promised to be seen little in his company during the remainder of the voyage.

Brady's death was the sensation of the next morning, and subsided with the storm by noon.

Greyson finished his narrative, as Colonel Brady had done ten years ago that night on the Atlantic liner. As he did so one of our company fell heavily forward from his chair upon the floor. It was the Hon. David Ryerson, a financial citizen of rare public repute and fondly regarded by us all. We carried him to the divan and restored his faculties.

"What was it, old man," we inquired solicitiously, "was that tale of horrors too much for you?"

Pouring off a glass of cognac to steady his nerveless limbs he feebly said:

"Colonel Brady was my brother, the leading member of the Diamond Trust of Ryerson Brothers. Brady was our real name, but when Fessenden reappeared from Africa he wished to drop the old family title and call the stupendous business absorption which we organized Ryerson, after my Christian appellation. I did not trouble to question why. He had a humorous fancy for traveling under assumed names, and latterly had fostered a fresh affection for the one under which he was born, with the appendix Colonel, which he said he had earned in the rescue of Christendom. His means were literally unlimited and he bought in competing houses like second-hand furniture. He told me a very different story of the origin of his wealth from the true one; I was deceived and I agree with you that he deserved his fate,—you did right, Greyson, you did right. He had upon his person that night a belt containing a million dollars' worth of precious stones which he was bringing home from abroad and they went down with him. The loss of these was nothing, but I feared they were wrong in surmising the manner of his death, and that there might have been foul play: it was his method always to carry a small fortune about on his person despite my protests, which might have become known. He was sensitive and enjoyed the intimate physical presence of riches. I believe he would have liked to bathe in a mint of gold. I was right in my dread that he had died a violent death, but no other retribution could justly have culminated such a life."

We sat with white faces, tense with the dénouement of the weird tragedy. The midnight bells began to clank the death-rattle of the sinking century. A letter was handed in to Greyson postmarked Paris, with directions for delivery on the last night of the year. He tore it open, ran through it, then ground his teeth, dashing the crumpled paper to the floor. By this time we were strung up to hear and believe anything.

"Read it," he moaned, and one of us did so aloud. It was as follows:

"My dear Greyson: I hope you will receive this about the middle of the last night of Nineteen Hundred. If you do, it will recall a good deed of yours committed ten

years ago when three of you saved the life of——an
African Prince, do you remember him? I was the Prince
that night, altho I abdicted at the end of the voyage,
but thanks to the charming story of our friend Colonel
Brady I drew a salary of a million dollars for the brief
period of my reign. I knew that he carried diamonds
of great value, then in his stateroom through the chafing
weight of his belt, which I had inspected. By the law
of beauty I coveted them, but how by that law or the
stauncher one of private expansion was I to obtain them
and elude the search of the ship which would immediately
follow their loss?

"I shaped my plan out of his alluring adventures as I
listened, and adopted his African King for my father. The
bait seemed much to your liking, for you made a hearty
meal of it. Of course you and your friends could not visit
his stateroom after the tragedy to invoice his effects, without exposing the secret or implicating yourselves if you
were seen; but I could and did drop in there after leaving
you, and assimilated the precious stones.

"You can't trace me. I was so adapted for the occasion that I could not have been known by my own father—
Milto—and that was ten years ago. I've changed since
and am now a prodigiously rich and respectable citizen
in a certain opulent capital, I will not state whether of
Europe or America, though in tribute to the soaring spirit
of my countrymen I will say that I was born in a righteous
American home. I am, dear Greyson, in my own wide
sphere of banking and the general fraternity of trade, very
much the kind of splendid public figure that our lamented
companion Brady was internationally.

"Did my conscience ever afflict me? It might have done
so had I not been deeply schooled in a long evening of
Colonel Brady's morals. Altho I followed him upon the
voyage for the jewels I had no purpose against his life,

nor should I have taken it if my attempts on his wealth had failed, had I not learned from his lips the true principles of world commerce in which till then I had been a gentle novice. Since he could gain incalculable loot by the bounty of international ethics, why should I recoil from dipping a share out of his vessels with his own ethical instruments? No, my conscience never has troubled me, and I have since then gloriously succeeded along the track which he was kind enough to spread before my dazzled gaze.—And I contribute regularly to send out missionaries as pioneers of God and commerce.

"I fearlessly give you plenty of clues, you see; I am now traveling with my dear wife who is the daughter of one of your most distinguished countrymen, whose international ethics beautifully coincide with mine, and we are stunningly happy. For your courtly courtesy I thank you, its memory always softens me, it was a tribute to American soul; every one should be a king once in a while to learn what a gurgling fountain of affection there is in his fellowmen. I owe you a great deal. If you are ever in trouble—but I couldn't very well help you, could I?

"Your Gracious and Appreciating ex-Sovereign,

"THE AFRICAN PRINCE."

THE END.

Lightning Source UK Ltd.
Milton Keynes UK
UKHW022358261118
333019UK00015B/1735/P